SWINBURNE

BY

HAROLD NICOLSON

ARCHON BOOKS
1969

SBN: 208 00796 2
LIBRARY OF CONGRESS CATALOG CARD NUMBER: 69-19218
PRINTED IN THE UNITED STATES OF AMERICA

SWINBURNE

CONTENTS

"The great love of great things, the great scorn of small men, the strong tenderness of heart, the tender strength of spirit, which won for him honour from all that were honourable. Ready even in a too fervent manner to accept, to praise, to believe in worth and return thanks for it, he will have no man or thing impede or divert him, either for love's sake or for hate's."—SWINBURNE, *Blake*, p. 41.

CHAPTER I

SWINBURNE has hitherto been fortunate in his bio-
graphers. For it would indeed have been regrettable
if the life-story of one who, although surpassingly
strange, was yet so exquisite a gentleman, had been
marred from the outset by any ungentle handling. In
Edmund Gosse, Swinburne found a historian such as
the fates accord but rarely to the inheritors of fulfilled
renown. An intimate friend for over forty years, Sir
Edmund Gosse was able to enrich the *Life of Swinburne*
with that wide literary science and that velvet style
which have rendered him an unchallenged master of
critical biography : not only does the official life of
Swinburne display with delicacy and not without
frankness the many facets of this elusive subject, but,
what is infinitely more important, Sir Edmund Gosse
has once and for all set the key or tone for all future
study of the poet—for all study, that is, which may
lay claim to any seriousness. There are those who
regret that the gay and vivid colours of *Portraits and
Sketches* are not throughout reflected in the more
restrained pages of the official biography, and who
would accuse Sir Edmund Gosse of having poured

much water in his sacerdotal wine. Such criticism proceeds, perhaps, from a misapprehension of Swinburne's essential character, as well as from a faulty knowledge of the sense of values possessed by Sir Edmund Gosse. For of all poets Swinburne lends himself the most readily to caricature ; in no biography is it more easy, or more fatal, to miss, or to exaggerate, the point.

It must be admitted, of course, that the side-tracks and the blind-alleys in Swinburne's life and character are many and various, and that the main thoroughfare is sadly encumbered. It might be possible, for instance, without diverging too widely from the apparent landmarks, to portray Swinburne solely as some garish faun whirling lascivious through the drab decades of mid-Victorianism. Again, one might be tempted to treat the matter wholly pathologically and to furnish a picture of a half-epileptic, half-dipsomaniac, retiring finally to an inebriates' home at Putney, much as Coleridge sought the discipline of Mr. Gillman up at Highgate. There have been those already who, being obsessed by the fantastic in Swinburne, have exhibited him as no more than some chryselephantine marionette, with fluttering hands and, below, the famous patent-leather μαρμαρυγαὶ ποδῶν. There will be those, doubtless, who will one day explore the intricacies and causes of his non-existent sexual repressions, and will trace depressing and essentially erroneous analogies to Dr. Masoch or the Marquis de Sade. And lastly, and much more seriously, there are many even now who agree with Meredith in thinking him devoid of " an internal centre ", and who can conceive of him only as a mirror flashing to the light of other suns, as a bundle

of dried herbs blazing fierce and aromatic to the fire
of other people's inspiration.

It is this last method of approach which responds
most directly to the present reaction against Swinburne,
and which appears with frequency and in varying forms
in all recent critical estimates of his work.   Thus Mr.
Drinkwater, in his tender and conscientious study of
the poet, is distressed by what he calls " his mastery
over utterance " and the " fixity in the temper of his
language "—by the fact that the worst poetry of Swinburne is so disconcertingly similar to the best.   Even
M. Reul, that excellent commentator, is at moments
angered by Swinburne's lack of outline ; and persistent
is the accusation that this mass of poetry is so inconclusive as to be almost insincere.   Such opinions centre
round what is in fact the nucleus of present disesteem,
namely, that Swinburne, who to his contemporaries was
" the most exciting thing that ever happened ", appears
to our later generations as almost unutterably dull.   I
should be the last to deny that from any continuous
reading of his poetry a certain lethargy is apt to result ;
nor would I affirm that this is solely due to a transitory
fluctuation in taste.   It may be admitted from the outset that we shall find it difficult to-day to enter into
any sensitive relation with the whole of Swinburne's
work ; that there are lengthy passages in his verse to
which modern sensibilities can scarcely be expected to
respond.   But for this very reason an examination is
from the outset necessary of the causes which provoke
this feeling of repletion ; an analysis must be made of
these causes ; and some theory must be evolved which
may serve as a guide to what is " good " in Swinburne's
poetry and what is " bad ".   Such a theory will show,

I trust, that much of the present distaste for Swinburne
is due to purely accidental causes, such as his technique,
and that there does in fact exist in Swinburne an
" internal centre ", tenuous but intense, which, if once
realised, will give to his poetry an abiding interest and
a stimulating originality.

The constant interruption or incompleteness of full
sympathy between Swinburne and his reader can in
the first place be traced to faulty communication—to
the fact, that is, that he so frequently fails adequately
to communicate the full emotion which he has himself
experienced. It is not merely that Swinburne possessed
no sense of audience, it is also that his audience so rarely
attain to any sense of Swinburne. The cause of this
misunderstanding is predominantly to be found in the
interposition, or over-emphasis, of his technique. The
exaggerated enthusiasm which he inspired from 1867
to 1900 was due largely to the novelty of his music ;
to-day the tunes which he either invented or perfected
have lost their glamour and their surprise. To us, his
anapaests appear but as the " song of Circe and her
wine ", whereas to his contemporaries they were
welcome as a dash of sea-spray upon the brow. This
is in itself a serious loss in appreciation ; we are apt
to forget the great services which he rendered to
English prosody, and to criticise even his lack of
variation in the internal handling of his melodies.
But what is more important is that his insistent metrical
stress is liable, and to a damaging extent, to obstruct
communication.

In a sense, therefore, the difficulty of entering into
continuous and vigilant sympathy with Swinburne's
poetry arises not only from the familiarity but also

from the perfections of his prosody. The elaboration
of his metres and cadences, the anticipation which is
allayed or evoked by the satisfaction or disappointment
of aural expectancies, to-day produce, not a stimulating, but a narcotic effect, distract the reader's
attention, and render him dull to the meaning which
is really being conveyed. Take, for instance, a passage
such as the following :

> But afar on the headland exalted,
>   But beyond in the curl of the bay,
> From the depth of his dome deep-vaulted
>   Our father is lord of the day.
> Our father and lord that we follow,
>   For deathless and ageless is he ;
> And his robe is the whole sky's hollow,
>   His sandal the sea.
>
> Where the horn of the headland is sharper
>   And her green floor glitters with fire,
> The sea has the sun for a harper,
>   The sun has the sea for a lyre.
> The waves are a pavement of amber,
>   By the feet of the sea-winds trod
> To receive in a god's presence-chamber
>   Our father, the God.

A series of such stanzas produces a sort of hypnosis ;
the brain becomes so intent on the acoustic tremor
evoked that the words cease to have more than a purely
musical import. After a time the reader will pull himself together with an effort, emerge from his trance, and
re-read the words upon the page before him. The
reaction will, however, already have set in, and he will
already be alienated by what will appear to have been
almost a deception and a trick. He will then resent
the rhymes, the alliterations, and the assonances ; he
will be acutely susceptible to the absence of outline, the
vapid reiteration, and the distressing fluency. He will

understand what Swinburne meant when he referred to " the dulcet and luscious form of verbosity which has to be guarded against ". He will understand what Mr. Eliot meant when he called Swinburne's intelligence "impure". And he will lay the book down with a sigh of inertia. A few pages more, and the phenomenon will repeat itself ; let him take up one of the later volumes, and all element of surprise will have faded from the metre. Communication will by this process have been almost permanently severed.

It is true, of course, that were the modern reader, on emerging from a state of hypnosis to one of vigilance, to find in what he re-reads some co-ordinated signifi-cance, some organised meaning, the consequent reaction would not be so deterrent. But he is met at this stage by a further feature of the poet's lack of method, namely, an ill-organised use of images. Swinburne was content to inspire but nebulous thoughts of the things that his words stand for, nor did his manner of conception bring them into any very intelligible connection with one another. Mr. Eliot, to say nothing of the Symbolists, has shown us that any obvious co-ordination of images is in fact unnecessary for the evocation of a deep and immediate emotional response. What *is* necessary, however, is the con-viction that for the poet himself the images which he uses are in consecutive harmony with the experience he conveys ; given that conviction, the reader is all too glad to evolve his own interpretations, to weave his own allusions and associations. But the images of Swinburne are so perfunctory, so often dictated by mere sound-coincidence, that this essential conviction is not communicated. The reader is thus dissatisfied

at feeling that no further interpretation is either
required from himself or essayed by the poet, and
this dissatisfaction with what is, after all, largely a
matter of technique becomes fused and confused into
a criticism of value. Which is a mistake.

To illustrate my meaning I shall take at absolute
random two stanzas of Swinburne, in which this flaccid
use of images is only too apparent :

> Or haply, my sea-flower, he found thee
>   Made fast as with anchors to land,
> And broke, that his waves might be round thee,
>   Thy fetters like rivets of sand ?
> And afar by the blast of him drifted
>   Thy blossom of beauty was borne,
> As a lark by the heart in her lifted
>   To mix with the morn ?
>
> By what rapture of rage, by what vision
>   Of a heavenlier heaven than above,
> Was he moved to devise thy division
>   From the land as a rest for his love ?
> As a nest when his wings would remeasure
>   The ways where of old they would be,
> As a bride-bed upbuilt for his pleasure
>   By sea-rock and sea ?

A passage such as this, and there are countless other
passages which are equally typical, explains what might
be loosely called Swinburne's lack of consecutive grip,
a defect which differentiates his method from that of
so great a contemporary as Tennyson.

It is not, however, merely the narcotic quality of his
melody, nor the uninterpretative manner of his thought,
which ·to-day obstruct complete sympathy between
Swinburne and his reader. The absence of continuous
response to his poetry is due largely to the fact that
Swinburne was different from most human beings,
that he was undeniably eccentric, that between him

and the reader there is no sufficient basis of common interest. To his contemporaries this suspension of sympathy was not noticeable, since they were carried away by the purely destructive quality of Swinburne's inspiration, by the fact that, topically and incidentally, he was in full revolt. This brigandage aspect of the poet is now less apparent, and we observe only that his attitude towards existence was, to say the least, uncommon. It may well be that he envisaged " a life less thick and palpable than ours " ; but some of us will be tempted to exclaim, as M. Milsand exclaimed of Browning, " Quel homme extraordinaire, son centre n'est pas au milieu ".

It will be said, of course, that all poets differ from the average, and that to attribute to this difference an interruption of communication is to advance a theory which could be at once disproved by citing, for instance, the relation constantly and continuously established between the reader and Shelley. It becomes necessary therefore to decide whether the abnormality (using the word strictly as meaning a departure from the norm) of Swinburne is of some quality distinct from that of most other poets. Such a distinction can certainly, and should certainly, be made. For Swinburne is not a universal but a specialist poet ; he does not often enlarge the areas of human experience, he generally restricts them ; his method essentially is exclusive and not inclusive. But this alone would not suffice to any important extent to limit communication : there have been many admirable specialist poets with whom our sympathy is completely satisfactory. It must be shown, therefore, that Swinburne's specialisation was of so personal and so eccentric a kind that the average man can respond to it intermittently only and by a muscular effort of the will. The fact must also be emphasised that this eccentricity was of a very particular quality, of a quality unterrestrial, almost astral. This impression is only superficially due to his appearance, nor is it intended to refer to his sexual nature, which, in so far as it developed, was comparatively healthy. Still less does it derive from such curious contrasts as his causeless excitement and his causeless lethargy, his violence and his docility, his republican fervour and his patrician conduct. Such eccentricities could find their echo in many hearts. But there is some peculiar quality or defect in Swinburne which is so inexplicable and recondite that it segregates him from the rest of his kind, and establishes a wide gulf between what is of convincing interest to him and what to us. This quality can best be illustrated by two of its major symptoms, namely, by his arrested development and by his imperviousness to impressions.

It is a daring but not untenable paradox to contend that Swinburne's emotional receptivity began to ossify in 1857, that is, in his twenty-first year. The experiences which he had by then absorbed became his future attitudes : all subsequent experiences were little more than superficial acceptances or, as his passion for babies, special kinds of belief. The sea, the sun and wind had been absorbed in childhood ; with Eton came Sophocles, Sappho, the *Birds* of Aristophanes, Catullus, the Elizabethans, Landor, Hugo, Mary Queen of Scots ; during his first year at Balliol there flamed for him Mazzini and the detestation of Napoleon III. This strange assortment remained throughout his life the essential stimulus : there was no stimulus after 1857 that became really essential. It is apposite to note that in November of that year began his connection with the Pre-Raphaelites, and that it is not impossible that during the same summer he first read Baudelaire. Both of these tremendous forces affected him for a moment : but who could contend that they penetrated to his inner consciousness or created any permanent attitude ? How can it be denied that if it had been at Eton that he experienced Rossetti or the *Fleurs du Mal* his whole development would have been profoundly and continuously different ? The conviction therefore is imposed that in this we are faced by a phenomenon, and that some callosity began from 1857 onwards to block Swinburne's emotional receptivity until, by the age of thirty-four, he became quite incapable of reacting to the stimulus of any new experience.

These instances of arrested development receive further confirmation when we consider Swinburne's strange imperviousness to impression, or, as some might say, his temperamental lack of observation. He has been called the " Laureate of the Sea ", and there can be no question that the sea was the most readily available of all his stimulations. But even this inspiration, though continuous and intense, was not various : we respond to his sea-poems mainly because of their fine symbolic application, mainly because he gives so high an interpretative significance to the lustral quality of flowing waters. But it cannot be denied that his experiences of the sea remained, in their essence, those of boyhood, and that even in such a poem as " The Garden of Cymodoce " there is little evidence of adult receptivity. Hence the stock epithets and phrases (the simile of the " foam-flowers of the sea " must occur at least two hundred times in his poetry), and hence a certain languor, on our part, of response. One instance will suffice to illustrate this contention. In the summer of 1855 Swinburne at the age of eighteen was caught in a storm between Ostend and Dover : although in the years that followed he must have seen endless other storms, it is always the storm of 1855 to which he refers ; it figures throughout his verses ; it figures in an elaborate prose simile for the genius of Victor Hugo ; it figures again in the volume of poetry which he published in his sixty-eighth year. Surely such imperviousness discloses a nervous system of surpassing eccentricity !

If it be agreed, therefore, that Swinburne possessed a quality of abnormality distinct from that with which most poets are endowed, it may then be asked why such abnormality should affect our full appreciation of the poet, or the sensitive relation between him and the reader. The answer is, doubtless, that it should not, but that it does ; that the sense of some obstruction in free communication inevitably arises ; that although, so to speak, this obstruction exists only on one line of communication, yet it acts as a buzzer which disturbs the rest ; and that once the obstruction can be located and defined, then that particular line of communication can be rejected, and the others will ring clear enough. To achieve such an isolation is the purpose of this monograph, and particularly of this chapter. But it is not denied that such restricted communication cannot but bring with it a sense of dissatisfaction, a sense, above all, of wastage. An age may come when men will again enter readily into a sensitive relation towards the whole of Swinburne's work ; but for the present, if we can establish such a relation only with a portion of that work, much pleasure and much profit will accrue.

I have endeavoured hitherto to indicate some of the causes which have induced the depressing theory that Swinburne is dull. I have described this impression as due partly to the narcotic effects of his melody, partly to the lack of co-ordinated meaning in his images, but chiefly to the absence in his poetry of any wide basis of common experience. This exclusive quality of Swinburne's work has been still further analysed as being intensively specialist, and as deriving from a very distinctive abnormality of temperament ; this abnormality in its turn has been illustrated by two connected symptoms, that of his arrested development and that of his imperviousness to impressions ; and finally it has been indicated that, although by thus isolating the main obstruction which disturbs communication a more sensitive relation may be established towards part of Swinburne's work, yet a distressing loss and wastage will from such a process undeniably, but inevitably, result.

Having thus disengaged the unreality of Swinburne, it becomes necessary to examine his essential reality, to discover if possible what in fact constituted his " internal centre ". In a sense, of course, the true biography of Swinburne is the story of his writings. " Knowing as you do ", he wrote to Clarence Stedman, " the dates and sequences of my published books, you know every event of my life." This statement is in no way a gesture of affected modesty or self-protection :

for him, at least, it was the literal truth. He was so little self - conscious, that for long stretches of time he became almost unconscious ; the outside world flickered but vaguely for him as something wholly secondary, wholly unrealised, wholly incidental. In the foreground was always literature ; his only permanent excitement was that which he derived from books. There were moments, there were indeed long periods, when his only vital experience was a literary experience, and when he derived from such sources as Victor Hugo or the Elizabethan dramatists a stimulation which was something far wider and more intense than merely cerebral excitement. Such a condition of susceptibility may well be abnormal ; but assuredly it was not insincere, and undeniably it is not dull. In fact, when connected with other essential constituents of his psychology this symptom is one of real interest. And I think that it can be so connected.

The frequent statement that Swinburne derived his inspiration from literature and not from life leads to a certain confusion of thought, and to the mistaken criticisms that he was " derivative " and " unreal ". The feelings provoked in Swinburne by a work of art were just as direct, as real, and, I would add, as original, as the feelings provoked in Wordsworth by the contemplation of nature. It is important, moreover, to realise that this almost abnormal sensibility to the work of others is closely connected with his impulse of hero-worship, an impulse which in its turn is part of that submissiveness which was one of the two main constituents of his character. For the " internal centre " of Swinburne was, I am convinced, composed of two dominant and conflicting impulses, namely, the impulse towards revolt and the impulse towards submission. It is his exquisitely sensitive adjustment to the tension between these two impulses, between what psychologists would call "the instinct of self-assertion" and "the instinct of self-abasement", which constitutes his most original contribution to human experience, and which is therefore the real essence of his genius.

This statement, which is in fact the main thesis of my study, will require further examination, and will necessitate some analysis of the peculiar quality of Swinburne's revolt as well as of the no less singular nature of his submission. It has already been shown that he was curiously detached from ordinary human activities. Shelley alone of poets, though with greater self-consciousness, was equally disembodied. Swinburne quivers solitary, tremulous, aloof—as some lone sea-gull above the waves. The simile occurs again and again throughout his poetry; nor can the sweep, the purity, and the freedom of his inspiration be conveyed by any more vivid or appropriate symbol. This identification of himself with something bright and white and liberated illumines many a passage in his poetry which might otherwise appear incidental or obscure. It was not, however, merely the aloofness of a sea-bird which appealed so insistently to his imagination, it was, predominantly perhaps, the quality of liberation and escape. The ultimate freedom shone always for him as the sea and the sun-lit air above the sea: this, symbolically, was his constant aspiration. And meanwhile he strained and fluttered vehemently against the bars.

This hatred of imprisonment, this obsession almost

of claustrophobia, can be traced throughout the course of his life and literary production. There are the sudden escapades of his otherwise acquiescent childhood ; the mutinous moods of his last year at Eton ; the hysterical outbursts at Balliol. His early manhood was but a constant defiance of circumstances, a hectic search after new worlds to startle or to defy. Again and again we find him tilting wildly at windmills, attacking conventions which had already ceased to exist. Nor was this, to him, of any consequence : for what he loved was revolt only for the sake of revolt. And then in the end came Watts-Dunton and Putney, and the fine fire of mutiny was dimmed to a little lambent flame of wistfulness.

As a counterpart to this volcanic violence there stands his curious docility : an apparently causeless revolt matched by an apparently causeless submission : for submission also he loved as an absolute quality, and for its own sake alone. Thus whereas Swinburne was always escaping, yet he never ran away. It was not only to his parents, to Jowett, to Rossetti, to Landor, to Hugo, to Mazzini, or to Watts-Dunton that he manifested this strange subservience. There were moments, and less creditable moments, when he would abandon himself to his own submissiveness as to some delicious and excruciating pleasure. It was perhaps the sublimation of this complex which produced his hero-worship, and it was certainly in this form that he endeavours to justify it. There is a passage in his study of Blake, a strangely autobiographical volume, which illustrates exactly how Swinburne himself tried to envisage this curious constituent of his own character :

Intolerant he was by nature and to a degree noticeable even among freethinkers and prophets ; but the strange forms assumed by this intolerance are best explicable by the singular facts of his training—his perfect ignorance of well-known ordinary things and imperfect quaint knowledge of much that lay well out of the usual way. He retained always an excellent arrogance and a wholly laudable self-reliance ; being incapable of weak-eyed doubts or any shuffling modesty. His great tenderness had a lining of contempt—his fiery self-assertion a kernel of loyalty. No one, it is evident, had ever a more intense or noble enjoyment of good and great works in other men—took sharper or deeper delight in the sense of a loyal admiration ; being of his nature noble, fearless, and fond of all things good ; a man made for believing.

All this may not be very apposite to Blake, but it is singularly apposite to Swinburne. It is only by emphasising his impulse for revolt and his impulse for submission that we can attain to any consistent realisation of his character. It is only by constantly referring his poetry to these two dominant characteristics, or rather to the conflict or balance between them, that we can evolve any useful theory of his literary value.

It will be admitted, I presume, that the most durable of all Swinburne's works are *Atalanta in Calydon*, the " Hertha " group of *Songs before Sunrise*, and the second series of *Poems and Ballads of 1876*. In all these works a perfectly co-ordinated balance between revolt and submission is conveyed. *Atalanta* predominantly is perhaps the supreme product of the poet's genius. In this poem the faults of communication noticed in the earlier part of this chapter cease to obtrude. The experiences which was fused into this drama are in the first place various. There is the

stimulus of sun and light, the stimulus of Sophocles
and Sappho ; the stimulus of youth, of that particular
form of lithe virginity to which Swinburne's temperament was so curiously attuned ; the stimulus of boyish
mutiny and boyish adventure ; the stimulus of fear
and pity ; the stimulus of muscular strength ; the
stimulus of melody ; the stimulus of freedom. These
present to the reader a sufficient basis of common
experience, and communication is thus established.
These experiences in their turn produce, both in the
poet's mind and in that of the reader, a whole connexus
of memories and emotions. In this instance, however,
Swinburne's method is not exclusive but inclusive ;
there is a continuous widening and not a continuous
narrowing of experience ; there are no repressions, his
imagination becomes formative, the impulses evoked
are connected with other impulses and fused into an
ordered whole ; he attains to a stable poise, a poise all
the more effective since it culminates in a perfect balance
between pity and terror and the κάθαρσις is provoked.
But in its essence this poise is in fact one between
revolt and submission ; it is the exquisite skill with
which both these impulses are brought to the quivering
point of equilibrium that causes so deep an emotional
response. The very fact that the central chorus, with
its sudden exaggeration of the element of revolt, is the
one faulty passage in the whole poem, indicates that it
is the balanced tension between the two impulses, and
not the mere statement of the impulses themselves,
which produce the passionate force of *Atalanta*. The
truth of this contention is, I think, demonstrated if we
compare *Atalanta* with *Erechtheus*. The latter play is
conducted upon a higher plane and in a more rarefied

atmosphere ; but the balance between revolt and submission is not similarly achieved since the latter element is throughout given a more insistent predominance. Thus we experience on reaching the crisis a less urgent necessity for emotional adjustment, and the ultimate solution produces a less satisfying emotional relief.

A similar deduction can be drawn from a comparison between the " Hertha " group of *Songs before Sunrise* and the earlier poems embodied in that volume. For whereas those verses which, in my analysis of the book, I shall call " Poems of the Risorgimento ", are concerned predominantly with revolt and thus suggest " a whirlwind in a vacuum ", the later and more philosophical poems do indeed deal with this conflict between revolt and submission, and achieve and inspire thereby a far more important emotional problem and adjustment.

The second series of *Poems and Ballads* stands in a somewhat singular relation to the rest of Swinburne's poetry. Hitherto his best work had been based on the perfection of balance between the two dominant impulses of his temperament, whereas those poems in which one or other of these impulses was unduly stressed had fallen short of this perfection. In the volume of 1876, however, both the two impulses are toned into a minor key, the old revolt becoming but a vague wistfulness, the old submission but a pathetic acquiescence. There is thus a gentle equilibrium between the two rather than an acutely balanced tension, and the circumstances that his technique during the same period reached the highest point of development, renders the whole volume the most organic of all his symphonies. These circumstances

constitute no disproof of my thesis : for the negative
equilibrium of the 1876 volume conveys a wholeness
of impression only slightly less important than the
acutely positive tension of *Atalanta*. They are both
convincing, since they derive from Swinburne's
" internal centre ".

The converse of this argument applies, I think,
with equal conviction. Those of his poems, as
for instance *A Century of Roundels*, which do not
reflect these central impulses are merely of prosodic
interest : those in which, as in the first series of
Poems and Ballads, one element is emphasised at the
expense of the other, fail to inspire any permanent
conviction ; while those again in which the tension
between submission and revolt is apprehended but not
fully exploited, possess an interest greater perhaps than
their intrinsic worth or reputation.

This introduction may suffice to indicate, and
perhaps to justify, the method which it is proposed
to follow and the interpretation which will be placed
upon the value of Swinburne's experience. My thesis,
which will merely be implicit in this treatment of the
poet, is that his experiences were far more important
and direct than is usually supposed ; that, owing to his
arrested development, only those experiences, however,
which he acquired before his twenty-first year penetrated beyond the stage of emotions and became
attitudes ; that the most important of these attitudes
was his acutely sensitive relation towards the tension
between revolt and submission ; that only when he
was dealing with these two dominant impulses, and
not when he was dealing with those special forms of
belief which constituted his later experiences, was his

imagination at all formative ; and that these considerations, while they explain why so much of Swinburne's work provokes no response, and illustrate incidentally his deficient power of communication, may also serve as at least a temporary standard for the valuation of the vast bulk of poetry which he composed.

The elaboration of this theme will entail some manipulation of the analytical survey which is essential to this particular series. I trust, however, that this manipulation, in spite of the guide-book character of this monograph, will not be unintelligible. A further, and, it may be thought, a more unfortunate necessity imposed by such an initial thesis is that it entails a very detailed treatment of the years from 1838 to 1857 and a very cursory treatment of the years that followed. A similar exercise of arbitrary construction will be noticed in the space devoted to the several works. Why, for instance, should more notice be taken of *Chastelard* than of *Bothwell*, why should *The Queen Mother* figure with greater prominence than the *Odes to Victor Hugo* ? My answer to this again is that it is only by concentrating upon the complete experience, upon Swinburne's " internal centre ", that we may hope, within the limits of a monograph, to convey some conception of what Swinburne really was. For that, after all, is a conception which it is desirable to convey.

CHAPTER II

JUVENILIA, 1838–1856

WE are wont nowadays to give to the childhood of our men of genius a greater prominence than was at one time customary.

This biographical habit becomes, in dealing with Swinburne, a psychological and critical necessity. It is not only that the early years of Swinburne stand in a curious contrast to his subsequent life and habits, are refreshingly average and active : it is predominantly, as I have just indicated and must repeat, because Swinburne was throughout his life abnormally obtuse to external impressions, that at a comparatively early age he became strangely impervious to any new idea or any fresh experience. His intelligence was already lavishly furnished before he reached full manhood, and it was exceptional in him thereafter to admit to the mansions of his mind any more modern contrivance or conception. He would listen, as always, with a rather vacant courtesy, a half-unconscious smile of self-preoccupation playing around his elfin lips, waiting patiently, like a well-behaved child, until one of the old and intimate stimulations should arrive ; and then, as George Meredith once said to Mr. Desmond MacCarthy, he would become " as an

ocean lashed into a tempest by a sigh ", or " at
the turn of the switch the whole town would be
suddenly ablaze with electricity ". The very rapidity
and intensity of Swinburne's response to those few
stimulations which he accepted, his strange persistent
concentration upon what, after all, were but a limited
number of impressions, the curious extent to which
his development was so early arrested, necessitate a
careful scrutiny of his early circumstances, of that
comparatively short period when his personality was
still sufficiently malleable to receive the impress of
the die. For there can be no doubt whatsoever that
Swinburne's more acute impressions were absorbed
during his first eighteen years : at Bonchurch, at Eton,
at Balliol, and in Northumberland. His subsequent
impressions were either derivative or were mere
artificial and deliberate forms of belief.

His own lineage was a point of pride to Swinburne,
and on occasions it became a point of vanity. It
delighted him extremely to picture his ancestors as a
fierce succession of border barons, merging, at the time
of the Dutch conquest, and with some suddenness, into
Catholics, Jacobites, and Exiles. It was pleasurable,
but not perhaps quite accurate, to describe how they
had given their blood " like water and like dust " for
the Stuarts. " I think that you will allow ", he once
wrote to Edmund Gosse, " that when this race chose
at last to produce a poet it would have been at least
remarkable if he had been content to write nothing but
hymns and idylls for clergymen and young ladies to
read out in chapels and drawing-rooms." Nor did
he omit on occasion to emblazon his ancestral tree with
certain decorative but apparently fictitious ascendants.

He would speak quite frequently of the " French particles in my blood ", explaining that these particles derived from a de Polignac ancestress, and even, when unusually eloquent, from the Marquis de Sade. " Men ", he once wrote, " who have the lineal pulse of French blood in their veins and the traditional memories of French kindred and alliance in their hearts. . . ." And at one moment we find him referring, with what authority I know not, " to some fusions of Hotspur's lineal blood in direct descent ".

These innocent mystifications need not, of course, be taken seriously. While being in general the most truthful and accurate of men, he would similarly tell little transparent fibs about his age, indulging thereby in the quite harmless vanity of claiming a precocity which was not, in truth, justified by the hard facts of his literary development. He would tell these lies quite unblushingly, and, when corrected, would respond only with that childish and engaging smile. And yet this insistence on the dare-devil, or the un-English, elements in his ancestry is a not unpleasing symptom of that school-boy romanticism, that school-boy courage, which never left him ; of that unfailing impulse to kick, and very hard, against the pricks. Nor, as regards the main facts of his lineage, was Swinburne so very far from the truth. From the time of Edward II. the Swinburnes had figured among the gentry of Northumberland ; since Elizabeth they had been established at Capheaton ; and the baronetcy, after all, dates from 1660.

At the time of Swinburne's birth the holder of that title was Sir John Swinburne, the poet's grandfather, and a man who exercised upon Algernon a very

deep and decisive influence. For the old veteran of
Capheaton lived to the age of ninety-eight and was a
bare seventy-six when he first came to lay his nervous
hands upon the red curls of his distinguished grandson.
And Sir John Swinburne, alarming as he undoubtedly
was, possessed certain very rare and impressive
characteristics. He had been the friend of Voltaire and
of Mirabeau ; he had been an atheist, a Jacobin, and,
what was even more histrionic, a professing Jacobite.
He had tamed wild horses and loved exotic women,
and now he would walk with his grandson in the dense
shrubberies of Capheaton, or show him the French
folios in the library, or the Turners in the saloon,
discoursing in the manner of the Court of Versailles
about the rights of man, the social contract, or the
iniquities of tyrants, and recounting how he, at least,
had " repeatedly " rendered himself " liable to be
impeached and executed for high treason ". Assuredly
a grandfather after Swinburne's heart.

The poet's father, Admiral Charles Henry Swinburne, the second son of Sir John, comes down to us
as a far less symbolic figure. Upon him also Algernon
endeavoured in later years, with stories of Collingwood
and Canaris, of Navarino and Lady Hester Stanhope,
to throw the high light of adventure. But to us he
appears merely as a somewhat bewildered sailor, kindly,
red-haired, and irritable, with a healthy loathing for the
arts of literature and music, and a remarkable capacity
for the invention of ingenious mechanical devices.
Here at least Swinburne could justify his claim to be
" epigenetic ", for to him any mechanism, even in so
innocent a form as a soda-water syphon, remained for
ever a subject for fumbling thumbs and acute nervous

tension. More direct and recognisable was the heritage, physical and temperamental, which he drew from his mother. Lady Jane, daughter of the third Earl of Ashburnham, was a woman of the most elegant accomplishments and of the sweetest docility. Educated abroad, and predominantly in Florence, she would read French and Italian to her children, slurring the words softly in a sing-song voice, stressing unduly, as is the way with the Italian tongue, the accented syllables, and this with an intonation almost Slav in its deliberate languor.

It is this intonation which has crept into so much of Swinburne's poetry, and which, until he became over-excited, would lull his subsequent auditors into trances of rapturous enjoyment. And it was thus indirectly from Lady Jane that the young Oxford of the 'sixties derived the Swinburne drawl.

Although the whole of Algernon's childhood was spent either at Bonchurch in the Isle of Wight, at Capheaton in Northumberland, or at Ashburnham Place in Sussex, he was actually born, on April 5, 1837, in Chester Street, Grosvenor Place, London. A few months later the family moved to East Dene, Bonchurch, which Admiral Swinburne had rented for a term of years, and which was but four miles distant from Northcourt, the home of Lady Mary Gordon, sister of Swinburne's mother. The relations between East Dene and Northcourt were close and affectionate, and the children of both houses formed a frequent and competitive association, healthy, stimulating, and intensive. For, indeed, no nineteenth century childhood can have been more lavish or more serene than that of Swinburne. Intensely English, of course, and somewhat patriarchal; the smell of hot water cans and dried lavender ; the feel of starched collars on Sunday mornings ; the scent of warm phlox in walled gardens ; the acrid savour of sea-weed on the beach below. An impression of tall untidy trees behind one, of wide flat lawns in front, and then, beyond, the bright high curtain of the sea :

> The many-coloured joys of dawn and noon
> That lit with love a child's life and a boy's,
> And kept a man's in concord and in tune
> With lifelong music of memorial joys
> Where thought held life and dream in equipoise.

It was among such surroundings, " between the sea-cliff and the sea ", that Swinburne spent his childhood. Nor was he ever unconscious of his privilege, or forgetful in the feckless years that followed of those " all-golden gifts of dawn ", the gaiety, the health, and balance that had once been his,—" the glad live past that cannot pass away ". His childhood days, although sheltered, were not, however, entirely sedative. In the first place there was

> The sun to sport in and the cliffs to scale,
> The sea to clasp and wrestle with, till breath
> For rapture more than weariness would fail.

There were feats of daring, feats of endurance, and feats of skill. He was a fierce and excitable rider and would show off impetuously before his Gordon cousins. Accidents would follow (on one occasion of a serious nature), and on many a summer evening Algernon would creep back to the stables with his little white face lined with blood.

His education, meanwhile, was not entirely neglected. From his mother, as we have seen, he learnt French and

Italian. His knowledge of French was scholarly and profound : it was only as regards accent and intonation that it showed any deficiency. From her also he absorbed much knowledge of the more reputable English classics, and, what was more important, of the Bible—which great text-book of all English men of letters became one of the most important constituents of his style. It may be surmised, however, that his early reading at Bonchurch was intensive in character rather than extensive : his cousin, Lord Redesdale, dismissed it later as having been " but the veriest pap " ; and we know, at least, that Lady Jane had placed all novels upon the index, and that before he left for Eton she exacted from him a promise that he would never, whatever the temptation, consult the works of Byron. From his father, it appears, he absorbed but little enlightenment. We may well presume that there was a period during which the Admiral endeavoured to inculcate into his son those aptitudes for exact mechanical constructions at which he himself was such an adept ; but, as has been said, the fat stubby fingers of Algernon did not lend themselves to such dexterity. It appears, indeed, and not only from the continued childishness of his handwriting, that he suffered from some muscular affection of the wrist ; and in any case the attempts at carpentry must soon have been abandoned. There is a pleasant picture, however, of the Admiral striding down the shingle and casting an ecstatic pink baby into the surf ; and this thalassian gesture left an impression more indelible than the gentle culture of his mother ; than the ministrations of the Rev. C. F. Fenwick, rector of Brook, who had by then been called in to assist in the formation of Algernon's learning.

On the religious side the Admiral and Lady Jane were High Church Anglicans, deeply affected by the Oxford Movement. This influence, although there is reason to suppose that it survived in an attenuated form at Eton, and although it returned suddenly during his first two terms at Oxford, was completely swept away by the icy torrent of Balliol agnosticism; but at the moment it was powerful enough. " Of course," Swinburne recorded in later years, " I went in for that as passionately as for other things, *e.g.* wellnigh to unaffected and unashamed ecstasies of adoration when receiving the Sacrament."

The summer holidays would be spent in Northumberland, and it is Capheaton with its fresh batch of cousins and its opportunities for even more romantic feats of horsemanship and swimming which forms the background of a whole batch of reminiscent verses. That singularly haunting homesick poem, *The Tale of Balen*, written at Putney in his fifty-seventh year, is directly inspired by the memories of Northumberland, and by the poignant recollections they evoked. Mr. Watts-Dunton, for his part, did not think that Northumberland would in any way be good for Algernon, and was in fact indignant with Mr. Thomas Hardy for having suggested such a summer holiday. So all that the docile poet could do was to sit down sadly and write again about

> The joy that lives at heart and home,
> The joy to rest, the joy to roam,
> The joy of crags and scaurs he clomb,
> The rapture of the encountering foam
>   Embraced and breasted by the boy,
> The first good steed his knees bestrode
> The first wild sound of songs that flowed
> Through ears that thrilled and hearts that glowed
>   Fulfilled his death with joy.

It was Capheaton also which formed the background of that very foolish play *The Sisters*, a production which is of value only for its beautiful dedication to Lady Mary Gordon, and for the wealth of autobiographical detail which it contains. For in Reginald Clavering, as also to a less extent in Reginald Harewood of *Love's Cross-currents*, Swinburne has drawn what he sincerely hoped was an accurate portrait of the artist as a young man. The general tone of Bonchurch, Northcourt, and Capheaton is here very adequately reflected : there are the grown-ups, closely related to each other, who discourse sedately in the morning-room ; there are the younger people, also closely related, who tease each other behind the herbaceous border ; there are the family jokes and jealousies, the amateur theatricals ; there is even the Admiral's work-shop in the garden. For the purpose of his ridiculously lurid drama, Swinburne has represented himself and his cousins as being already of age (Reginald Clavering has just returned heroically wounded from the field of Waterloo), but the whole atmosphere of the piece is a schoolroom atmosphere : Reginald Clavering is really Swinburne at the age of sixteen. As such, this character-sketch is interesting and vivid enough. For there are indications that, for all the gay sanity of his boyhood days, Swinburne was even at that date not wholly unassailed by complexes. The very fact that Reginald Clavering is represented as a young veteran of Waterloo, modest but heroic, is in itself a reflection of what was Swinburne's earliest disappointment. As a child he had longed to be a lighthouse-keeper, but from the age of nine his ambition centred upon the army. On leaving Eton he made a determined effort to enter the Dragoons ; the proposal, even at that date when his health was comparatively stable, was clearly grotesque. The Admiral, as was only natural, refused. The disappointment for Algernon was as galling as it was permanent : at the moment, which coincided with the news of Balaclava, he proceeded to scale Culver Cliff, demonstrating by that amazing feat that if he could not be a light dragoon he could at least be reckless. And twenty years afterwards, when discussing his increasing deafness with Edmund Gosse, he concluded quite naturally, " So that, after all, I suppose I should not have done well as a soldier." This curious obsession, this pathetic virility complex, is significant not only of Swinburne's persistent inability to realise with any actuality either himself or his surroundings, but also of his continual struggle against the incomplete physical development which separated him from the normal male. It was only in his early manhood that these disabilities developed into anything really afflicting, but even as a boy, even as a child, his small stature, his strange elfin appearance differentiated him from those other children whose accomplishments he forced himself to imitate and whose capacities he could not cease from envying. That he was vaguely conscious of this perplexing differentiation, that he was aware in some dull smarting way that the Gordon girls looked upon " Cousin Hadji " as something rather feminine and odd, is apparent from more than one passage in *The Sisters*. For Reginald Clavering, justified now triumphantly by the wound of Waterloo, is referred to slightingly by Cousin Anne as an " all but girl-faced godling in the hall ", is mentioned by Sir Arthur Clavering as having been

> Till now
> The unlucky boy—the type of luckless youth,
> Poor fellow—

and is addressed by the love-struck Mabel in a tone of very curious reminiscence :

> Well, you always were the best to me ;
> The brightest, bravest, kindest boy you were
> That ever let a girl misuse him—make
> His loving sense of honour, courage, faith,
> Devotion, rods to whip him—literally
> You know—and never by one word or look
> Protested.

The above suggestion that Swinburne was bullied and beaten by his girl cousins is not confirmed in the book which Mrs. Disney Leith published subsequently upon the boyhood of " Cousin Hadji ". But other traits of Reginald Clavering are abundantly reflected in that pleasant little volume. For the picture of the boy Swinburne, as indeed the final picture of the man Swinburne, is emphatically that of some one " brave and bright and kind " ; of a character generous and impulsive—

> Just a hot-head still—
> The very schoolboy that I knew you first
> On fire with admiration and with love
> Of some one or of something, always.

Nor would these words apply with less undeniable accuracy to the Swinburne even of " No. 2 The Pines " ; to Swinburne even at the age of seventy-one.

When twelve years old he was sent to Eton, where he remained for almost four years. Lord Redesdale, to whose charge Algernon was entrusted, has furnished Sir Edmund Gosse with a very charming record of his strange young cousin's first arrival. He stood there, straight-eyed and unselfconscious, looking " strangely

tiny ", and hugging a huge volume of Bowdler's Shakespeare, from which protruded a blue ribbon terminating
in a little button of Tonbridge marqueterie.   An exotic
figure certainly, with his huge shock of carrot hair and
his little pallid face, dancing along buoyant and yet
aloof, or curled up under the wide open boards of some
folio in the boys' library in Weston's yard.   Unlike
Shelley in similar circumstances, Swinburne was not at
all unhappy at Eton.   It is true that he mixed but little
with his companions, that he took no part in their
games, and that it was only during the summer half
that Cuckoo Weir and Upper Hope afforded an occasion
to demonstrate that he also was not entirely devoid of
physical prowess.   But in spite of his small size and
his egregious appearance, in spite of the fact that he
was currently known as " Mad Swinburne ", in spite
of the fact that to the more charitable he seemed but
an " inspired elfin ", and to the more conventional, such
as Michael Hicks-Beach, he figured as " a horrid little
boy with a big red head and a pasty complexion ", yet
his indomitable courage, his unfailing good manners,
the level dignity of those straight green eyes, inspired
his would-be tormentors with a certain caution, with a
certain rather astonished respect.   " There was something ", records Sir George Young, one of his few
schoolboy friends, " a little formidable about him."
As the years passed he and Lord Redesdale, his whilom
protector, drifted apart :   one may conceive that
Bertram Mitford was a very successful schoolboy.
Swinburne, for his part, was not, even at his books,
beyond the average :   he obtained the Prince Consort's
prize for French ;   on one occasion he was " sent up
for good " in Greek elegiacs ;   but on the whole he

became, and in spite of much subsequent furbishing remained, but a second-rate classical scholar, of whom his tutor, Mr. Joynes, was in no sense inordinately proud. Yet, as has been said, he was not unhappy during those four years at Eton, and looked back to his schooldays with an affection which contrasts curiously with his ultimate loathing of Oxford. Of Eton, in his old age, he could write as follows :

Still the reaches of the river, still the light on field and hill,
Still the memories held aloft as lamps for hope's young fire
    to fill.

But of Oxford in after years he could write only in terms of strident abuse.

His holidays were spent, as always, either at Bonchurch or at Capheaton. They were not devoid of a few salient incidents. In the summer of 1849 he was taken by his parents to the Lakes, and had the good fortune to visit Wordsworth six months before the latter's death. The aged Laureate was attentive to the boy, told him the story of General Wolfe reciting Gray's *Elegy*, was in fact so kind, so venerable, and so famous that the young Etonian dissolved into tears of ecstasy. On another occasion George Young came to stay at Bonchurch, and later in the year there was a visit to Ashburnham Place and long rides in the woods with his cousin Lady Katherine. A year later there appeared at East Dene a Signora Fronduti, who helped him much with his Italian and who read aloud to him the *Inferno* and the *Paradiso*. And one evening he was taken to St. James's Place to visit Samuel Rogers — at that period a happy feline old man of eighty-seven. The distinguished poet, host, and banker, who even to Byron had seemed worn with years, placed his two

D

hands upon the flaming head of Algernon with the remark, " I prophesy that you will be a poet too." By which utterance young Swinburne, who liked old men in principle and old poets in particular, was highly stimulated.

By the spring of 1853, with the advent of his seventeenth year, Swinburne showed signs of restlessness. His tutor, Mr. Joynes, complained of idleness and lack of discipline : these symptoms increased during the summer term, and " in consequence of some representations " (I quote Sir Edmund Gosse) Algernon did not return to Eton in September. There followed two and a half years of private tuition. For a time he worked with the Rev. J. R. Woodford in the Vicarage of Kempsford in Gloucestershire. In July of 1856 he paid an isolated visit to Germany, travelling via Wiesbaden to Würzburg and Nuremberg in the company of his uncle George Ashburnham. It was on his return voyage, while crossing from Ostend to Dover, that there occurred the thunderstorm to which I have referred in my first chapter as being one of the most exploited of Swinburne's rare experience of nature.

Such, then, were the outward circumstances of the poet's life from his childhood until his nineteenth year. A jejune and meagre narrative, perhaps, and one that would throw but little light upon the poetic development of any one less eccentric. Indeed, he experienced at Eton but few of those formative reactions which are the lot of ordinary schoolboys, yet what he did absorb remained with him throughout his life a constantly available stimulus. Predominant among his schoolboy experiences were those literary adventures which in after years became the real foreground of his life.

At home, as we have seen, his literary explorations were somewhat circumscribed : his mother would read him Beattie's *Minstrel*, and Charles Dickens and Wordsworth ; he himself would spend hours in the schoolroom over the *Lays of Ancient Rome* and his expurgated version of Shakespeare ; his grandfather up at Capheaton went further, and initiated him into the delights of early French romance ; but it was not till he fell in with Lamb's *Specimens of the English Dramatic Poets* that he discovered the theme which was to be the excitement of his youth, the inspiration of his middle years, the solace, and even then the excitement also, of his old age. " That book ", he once said to Sir Edmund Gosse, " taught me more than any other in the world—that and the Bible."

It was at Eton, therefore, and in the boys' library, that this taste for the Elizabethans and the Jacobean dramatists was confirmed and strengthened. We have already seen how he arrived at school clasping a Shakespeare : he left it with a knowledge of Shakespeare's contemporaries, precursors, and successors which in a boy of that age is assuredly amazing. Nor were his investigations confined to the beaten paths and easy handbooks of study : he borrowed *The Revenger's Tragedy* from his tutor ; he had read and re-read the Dyce edition of Middleton before going to Oxford. And the impression made upon him by what even then was his literary speciality was intensified during his holidays by the blood-and-thunder dramas which he and his cousins would enact in the drawing-room at East Dene or at Northcourt.

The Elizabethan dramatists were not, however, his only schoolboy discoveries. It is true that from his

classical studies, from the ordinary curriculum, he drew
no very personal excitement; it is curious, indeed, to
note how fortuitously his classical tastes were developed ;
it must have been by chance only that he happed at
school on Sappho and Catullus ; it was chance also
that led him, through a chorus in the *Birds*, to Aristophanes : the experience derived from forbidden fruit
is often penetrating, but how rarely is it permanent !
With Swinburne the persistence of these incidental
stimulations was amazing. In the wider field of
contemporary English literature his first enthusiasm for
" The Strayed Reveller " and " The Forsaken Mer-
man " was quenched by the chill negations of Matthew
Arnold's later lectures at Oxford. But Landor's
Hellenics, which he first discovered at Eton with
" inexplicable pleasure and a sort of blind relief ",
remained, as we shall see, a flaming experience for
ever. Another risen star of worship and of guidance
was Victor Hugo : *Notre Dame de Paris* he read in
1852, and in the following year *The Châtiments* produced
in him an enduring shock of admiration, " a sort of
rapturous and adoring despair ". The importance for
Swinburne of these literary experiences, almost the only
experiences which provoked in him any enduring
attitude, cannot sufficiently be emphasised and under-
lined.

Of the literary production of his schoolboy days
there is but little trace. Swinburne himself stated
that he destroyed every line written before he went up
to Oxford. We may question, perhaps, whether there
in fact existed very many lines for him to destroy : for
precocity, whatever he might pretend, was not among
his many endowments. There was some schoolroom

doggerel written for the amusement of his cousins ;
there were doubtless the scenario and perhaps the words
of more than one blood-stained drama in the manner
of Chapman ; and there still exists the manuscript of
a school piece dating from 1851 and entitled " The
Triumph of Gloriana ", in which a visit of Queen
Victoria to Eton is celebrated in the manner of Pope's
Iliad. A few critics, moreover, and notably Edward
Thomas, have been led astray by certain sententious
poems which appeared in *Fraser's Magazine* during
the years 1848 and 1849 over the initials A. C. S. The
fact that these poems were dated from the Carlton Club,
of which institution Algernon at the age of eleven can
scarcely have been even an honorary member, might
well have caused some suspicion ; but it was left to
the erudition of Mr. Thomas Wise to discover that the
author of these so-called " Juvenilia " was not Algernon
Charles Swinburne but Sir Anthony Cunningham
Sterling, K.C.B., late Major in the Highland Brigade.

For, indeed, the growth of Swinburne's own poetry
scarcely showed bud before he went to Balliol. The
soil was favourable from the outset, and the ground
was well prepared ; but the sap rose slowly, the season
was retarded, and when the blossom came at last it
burst upon an astounded world in a clustering riot of
white and scarlet. There may be those who will
question why, if this be so, I should have chosen at
such length to explore the circumstances of so unproductive a boyhood. My answer again is that the
sources of Swinburne's inspiration were so limited, his
experiences so few, his sensibility became so pre-
maturely callous. At Balliol, it is true, he learnt the
passion of liberty as well as the passion of the grape ;

but it is not on these themes alone that will be based his more enduring reputation. For the bright white flash which is the symbol of his genius arises from a wider and more radiant horizon ; and it is in his boyhood mainly that we can trace the essential quality of his experience, that we can discover the secret of his strange and incomplete emotional adjustment.

CHAPTER III

In Mr. Wise's admirable bibliography of Swinburne there are three photographs which were taken of the poet while at Balliol. Two of them are studio portraits : in the one he is leaning against an urn and pedestal, dressed in a braided tail-coat, grey trousers, and very shiny little shoes ; in the other he is seated beside a table with his left hand resting upon a book ; the third photograph, which is even more significant, represents him surrounded by his friends. From these three faded exhibits we can adequately reconstruct the personal appearance of Swinburne during his early years at Oxford. If further material be needed, reference can also be made to the astonishing portrait by William Bell Scott, recently bequeathed to Balliol by Mr. Raper. The fact that at that time he had not yet grown a beard throws into surprising contrast the upper and the lower sections of his face. The forehead, startlingly white and large under its masses of hair, squares well with the broad brows and the straight and level eyes below. The delicate thin nose, the long mobile upper lip, are not out of proportion either to the features above them or to the thick white column of neck on which the enormous head is poised. But the little loose lower lip, the tiny receding chin below, suddenly mar the beauty and the seriousness of the whole, giving to it a touch at once of the leonine and the elfin, a touch not of the grotesque so much as of the acutely disturbing. If such be the effect even of a photograph, the visual impression must in truth have been astonishing; for the first shock to the eye would have been one of flaming colour and twittering movement, and only gradually would the no less uncanny alignment and proportion of the features produce a vague surprise.

It is scarcely surprising that, being thus featured and contrived, Swinburne should at first have found himself a little shunned at Balliol, since that most excellent institution is apt to be unappreciative of all originality which is not of its own invention. They like their freshmen to reach them intelligent, well educated, and, above all, plastic; they will then, with kindly relish, exploit the originality for themselves; but actually to arrive odd is a most unpopular proceeding. It was not a wise thing to do even when Jowett, who could combine amazing sagacity with a distinct weakness for the eccentric, was all-powerful; but when, in January 1856, young Swinburne appeared at Balliol, Jowett had retired sulking to his tent, resenting, and with justice, the recent election to the Mastership of Robert Scott; and during the whole period of Algernon's residence at Oxford the silver tones of Jowett were not heard with any frequency in common-room.

Swinburne was not in general very sensitive to his surroundings, and it was but seldom that he became aware of the impression which he was producing, or failing to produce, on other people. But even upon the most impervious sensibility continued isolation in a crowd is apt to engender a cumulative effect, and the result for Swinburne was a very curious and wholly temporary reversion to the High Church Anglicanism of East Dene. The fading incense of the Oxford Movement still hung faintly about the damp stairways of Balliol, so soon, in their turn, to fall victims to the sprightliness of Mr. Waterhouse. And so for his first year at Oxford the poet, though not in all seriousness, would toy with the dead leaves of that fast receding cause, and would dabble, superficially perhaps, in Doctor Pusey, in Doctor Sewell of Radley College, and in the Caroline divines. Of all of which nothing remained to him a few months later beyond a firm regard for the prose, and even the verse, of Cardinal Newman. For his entry into the real life of Balliol was, when the moment arrived, to be essentially pagan.

The year 1857 is of outstanding importance in Swinburne's development. Until then, as has been noted, he had developed slowly : subjectively he had already absorbed at least two - thirds of his total experience, but objectively he had been comparatively static. He was born with a passion for the sun, the wind, and the sea ; at school he acquired a passion for the Elizabethan and Jacobean dramatists, a passion for Victor Hugo, and a passion for Walter Savage Landor. But until his twenty-first year these enthusiasms were but inchoate and voiceless. With his second year at Oxford the ores which he had for so long been extracting were thrown suddenly into the crucible ; other and baser metals were added ; and in a moment this strange amalgam glowed with a fiery incandescence, generating a white heat which quivered with scarcely undiminished intensity for more than fifty years. And the alchemists who assisted at this experiment were, curiously enough, John Nichol and William Morris.

In the third of the three photographs reproduced in Mr. Wise's bibliography—in the group, that is, of the members of the " Old Mortality Society "—the thin white face of John Nichol stands out from the rest in all its beauty and its self-assurance. Swinburne himself sits nervously on the edge of his chair, his short fat fingers clasping the cap upon his knee. Around him are grouped the remaining members of the Society : the bowed and oppressive brow of G. R. Luke; the more gentle brilliance of T. H. Green ; the thoughtful scholarship of Dicey ; the sturdy thoroughness of Bryce. But always the eye comes back to the clear-cut impassive face of John Nichol, serene, cynical, almost cruelly dominant. It is a face which it is difficult to reconcile with the subsequent career of one who became but Professor of English Literature at Glasgow, the author of *Hannibal*, and the compiler of some popular " historic tables ". For in those features one can recognise with certainty the cold keen blast of personality, of a personality which fanned the then smouldering embers of Swinburne's temperament into a sudden burst of flame.

There were certain other and more adventitious qualities in John Nichol which explain the rapid and complete ascendancy which in the early months of 1857 he obtained over Swinburne. In the first place, he was the latter's senior by two years (though not, incidentally, by six years as Swinburne subsequently

pretended) and had come up to Balliol a year before
the poet himself arrived. In the second place, he was
a man of the world and had already acquired much
experience in the less traditional atmosphere of
Glasgow University. And lastly, he was a free-thinker
and a republican, a man who had known J. S. Mill
and Kossuth, a man, finally, who already for five years
had been acquainted with Mazzini. The vague
republicanism which had been fermenting in the
excitable brain of Swinburne ever since those walks
with his grandfather at Capheaton, and which his
recent enthusiasms for Shelley, Landor, and Hugo had
turned into a more definite mental attitude, now found
for itself a local habitation and a name—became from
now onward personified in worship for Mazzini and
in blazing detestation of Napoleon III. In a moment,
under John Nichol's inspiriting influences, the Oxford
Movement was forgotten, and for ever discarded were
the Caroline divines. Above his mantelpiece he hung
a portrait of the would-be regicide Orsini, in front of
which he would dance solemn and solitary gavottes,
raising his hands from time to time " with gestures of
adoring supplication ". From that time onward he
would scream at the very mention of Napoleon. And,
finally, John Nichol encouraged him to drink.

I have been perhaps unduly influenced in my
estimate of Nichol by the overpowering impression
made upon me by that faded photograph of 1857.
Such few references to Swinburne as occur in the
published portion of the Professor's diary are in truth
unexceptional: " *June* 7. To Cumnor with Swinburne. Edgar Poe and green leaves. Chaucer in the
evening." What could be more bucolic ? Nor is

there anything particularly sinister in his early endeavour to convert Swinburne to the philosophy of Carlyle, or in his later attempts to reconcile him to the poetry and personality of Byron. Nor need it be forgotten that in the end John Nichol contrived to bore Swinburne. " I won't ", the latter wrote from Putney, " see Nichol again ! He spent the time reading his own stuff to me." But none the less the impression I have derived is distinct ; and it remains.

Be this as it may, it was Nichol indubitably who founded and inspired the " Old Mortality Society ", and it was his connection with this society which accounts primarily for Swinburne's feverish intellectual excitement of 1857. The first-fruits of the hectic mood induced and stimulated by John Nichol was the " Ode to Mazzini ", which, as Sir Edmund Gosse has convincingly shown, was written during the spring of that year. This ode was never published during Swinburne's lifetime, partly because the references to events in Italy had been rendered meaningless by subsequent developments, and partly because Swinburne, who was at that date studying Congreve, discovered shortly afterwards that to imitate Cowley's adaptation of the Pindaric metre was to follow a model both unscholarly and incorrect. An incomplete version of this ode was discovered in manuscript and privately printed by Mr. Wise in 1909 ; a more complete copy was, however, in the possession of the poet's sister, Miss Isobel Swinburne, and it is from this manuscript that the ode was reprinted among the *Posthumous Poems* of 1917.

This early " Ode to Mazzini " is not wholly a successful production. The movement of an ode is too measured to allow of continuous passages of sustained rhetoric, or to carry the rapid bursts of invective in which Swinburne never hesitated to indulge.   But none the less this, the earliest of his sustained efforts, is of considerable interest as indicating a certain immature ungainliness which he was able almost immediately to conquer, and as containing some personal mannerisms which he retained throughout his life.   The reiterant anapaests have not yet made their appearance, but the instinctive preference for the broad vowel sound of " i ", that bright white vowel of Swinburne at his best, already gives a personal colour to the piece.   The ugly hiatus, the accented past participle, the unintentional and jarring assonance, which figure so repeatedly in this early poem, soon disappeared in the clearer flow of his rapidly maturing melody ; the echoes of Shelley and of Matthew Arnold, the repeated echoes of Landor, were in his later verses fused into a more smooth and subtle harmonic texture ; but the absence of constructive power, the disregard of outline, which is the abiding weakness of Swinburne, is not more noticeable in this poem than in those of his poetic maturity ; while the hysterical adoration of his heroes (already in this poem Mazzini is " the Chief "), the scatologic abuse of their opponents, was an indulgence in the parade of which Swinburne remained a schoolboy to the age of seventy-two.   The following lines might well, with a little polishing, have figured in *Songs before Sunrise* :

> From priestly tongues that scathe with lies and vailing
>   The Bourbons' murderous dotard, sick of blood,
> To the " How long " of stricken spirits, wailing
>   Before the throne of God.

There is an echo of the real Swinburne in the lines :

> The winds, that fold around
> Her soft enchanted ground
> Their wings of music, sadden into song.

On the other hand the following passage, with its Matthew Arnold opening and its stumbling Shelleyan conclusion, could not by itself be identified as the work of one of the greatest original masters of English metrics :

> As one who dreaming on some cloud-white peak
> Hears the loud wind sail past him far and free,
> And the faint music of the misty sea,
> Listening till all his life reels blind and weak ;
> So discrownèd Italy
> With the world's hope in her hands
> Ever yearning to get free
> Silent between the past and future stands.
> Dim grows the Past and dull,
> All that was beautiful
> As scattered stars drawn down the moonless night :
> And the blind eyes of Scorn
> Are smitten by strange morn,
> And many-thronèd treason wastes before its might.

The spring and summer of 1857 were occupied in the preparation of an article on Congreve for a popular dictionary, on the publication of which Swinburne saw himself for the first time in print. He also at this time joined with John Nichol in competing for the Newdigate. The subject for the year was " The Temple of Janus ", and the prize was awarded, much to the indignation of Balliol, neither to Swinburne nor to Nichol, but to a Mr. Philip Worsley of Corpus. The manuscript of Swinburne's own endeavour has not been preserved. His real intellectual activity, however, still centred around the personality of John Nichol, and the debates and discussions of the " Old Mortality Society ".

Already the members of that Society were reacting against the predominant ascendancy of Tennyson, just as Tennyson's own apostles had in their time fought for Shelley against Byron.   It can scarcely be doubted that their objection to the Laureate arose rather from his official position and his generally accepted popularity than from any special hostility to his then published verse : the complacent and didactic passages of *The Princess* and *In Memoriam* may well have grated upon the nerves of John Nichol, who was not one of those who imagine that the beautiful need of necessity be good or tender.   It is difficult, however, except on the ground of wilful prejudice, to explain how the " Old Mortality " circle could have been blinded to the exquisite intensity of Tennyson's earlier poems, or how they failed to realise (as Swinburne himself realised) the smouldering passion of the still recent *Maud*.   For it must be recollected that the first four idylls, which would have explained and perhaps justified their ire, did not appear till two years later, and that the *Enoch Arden* volume was not published till 1864.   Yet it is the privilege and purpose of young and ardent coteries to disdain the appreciations of the vulgar, and the incense of " Old Mortality " was therefore swung with corybantic ecstasy, not before the shrine at Farringford, but at the feet of Young Italy, at the feet of Browning, and at the feet of John Ruskin ; in the performance of which devotion Swinburne not only intensified his existing propensities for hero-worship and republicanism, but added thereto the new stimulants of æstheticism and the analytical dramatisation of character.

His return from the Long Vacation, part of which he had spent with Nichol in the Hebrides, was signalised by an event of interest, but not, as some have supposed, of durable importance, in the history of his literary development. He met the Pre-Raphaelites. It will be remembered that William Morris had during the Long Vacation of 1857 been engaged upon the now faded decoration of the bays of the Union debating-room. He had come to Oxford for the purpose, and Burne-Jones and Rossetti had joined him in September. It was upon the damp and un-sized plaster of that ungainly room that under the cross-lights of Ruskinian trefoils the " crusade and holy warfare against the age " was to be initiated, the renascence of wonder was to be achieved. Morris up there on his ladder " doing " the roof, " making it something different from what it was " ; Burne-Jones equipped with " nothing but longing " intent upon the Arthurian legend ; Rossetti looming dominant, slangy, formidable. Besides, their keep was paid for by the Union authorities, and there was always beer, and puns, and poetry. So that at the beginning of the autumn term they were still engaged upon their labours ; and it was thus, on November 1, 1857, that Swinburne was simultaneously presented to the three of them by his friend Edwin Hatch of Pembroke. With Morris and Burne-Jones he soon established a close intimacy ; the friendship with Rossetti was of less rapid development. But, what is perhaps more important, Morris read aloud to him the manuscript poems of the *Defence of Guenevere*. Of these pieces one only, namely " Summer Days ", which had been published in the short-lived *Oxford and Cambridge Magazine* in October 1856, can have been already known to Swinburne. Their effect was instantaneous ; for it was Morris's adaptation of the early French romances, those books which he had merely fingered in the library at Capheaton, which seemed at the moment to open for Swinburne a fresh vista of inspiration and achievement.

His first experiment in this new manner was not long delayed. The members of the " Old Mortality " had for some months been considering by what means they could reach a public less restricted, but no less exclusive, than their own Society. The first number of *Undergraduate Papers* was issued in December 1857 : of this first number, only eighty copies were sold; after the third number, the scheme was abandoned. Swinburne himself contributed " four crudities " to *Undergraduate Papers*. In the first number he published an essay on Christopher Marlowe and John Webster, together with the first canto of a poem on " Queen Yseult ". In the second number he practised one of his favourite pranks of mystification by inserting a review of an imaginary work entitled " The Monomaniac's Tragedy and other Poems " by " Ernest Wheldrake " ; and to the third number he contributed an article on " Church Imperialism ", which he described subsequently as being a " terrific onslaught on the French Empire and its clerical supporters ".

Of these four contributions it is the poetry alone which need detain us, that " waif of verse " which figures as the last item in No. 1 as " Queen Yseult : Canto I." In after years, when he had come to repudiate and resent the short period when he had been directly under the influence of the Pre-Raphaelites, Swinburne endeavoured to dismiss this, his first published poem, as " some awful doggerel on the subject of Tristram ", and he begs Mr. Wise to

E

remember that these worthless rarities were " literally a boy's work—legally an infant's ". *Queen Yseult* is not, however, wholly doggerel, nor wholly to be dismissed even by the author in so irresponsible a manner. For in the first place the Canto published in *Undergraduate Papers* is merely the first of a projected ten cantos, of which six were actually composed by Swinburne during the early part of 1858, and privately printed in 1918 with an introduction by Sir Edmund Gosse. And in the second place the poem, although written under the direct influence of Morris's *Guenevere*, is, even as a *pastiche*, superior, as Morris admitted, to the original. *Queen Yseult* is not, moreover, the only production of Swinburne's William Morris period. Mr. Wise has discovered and printed privately certain other poems in the same manner, which had evidently been written in the winter of 1857–58.

The Christmas vacation of 1857, during which Swinburne was pursuing, with decreasing zest, the rather monotonous terzets of *Queen Yseult*, was spent at East Dene, where John Nichol came to visit him. The two undergraduates rode over one afternoon to Farringford and bearded the Laureate in his den. This visit is recorded by Tennyson in a famous passage : " Young Swinburne called here the other day with a college friend of his, and we asked him to dinner, and I thought him a very modest and intelligent young fellow. I read him (*Maud*), but what I particularly admired in him was that he did not press upon me any verses of his own." So that by January 1858 it was known in the Isle of Wight that the son of Admiral Swinburne was a professing poet.

The year 1858 was less exciting but more importantly

productive. Under the sagacious stimulus of Jowett, with whom he had now established relations of confidence, Swinburne paid more attention to his regular studies, and succeeded in obtaining a second class in Moderations and the Taylorian scholarship for French and Italian. The year is marked, moreover, by the foundation of a firm and lasting friendship with Pauline, Lady Trevelyan, his grandfather's neighbour at Wallington. For at this period the nonagenarian baronet was becoming a little intolerant of his vivacious grandson, and Swinburne tended to spend more and more of his time at Wallington, the home of the Trevelyans. With George Trevelyan, the nephew, he was never on terms of close companionship ; but Lady Trevelyan herself established over him a wise and sympathetic ascendancy, which lasted till her death in 1866. Almost daily Swinburne could be seen, as he was seen by W. B. Scott, riding through the heavy shrubberies on his way to Wallington, a pile of books strapped to his saddle, hatless, and chanting poetry as he went. And Lady Trevelyan, who was a close friend of Ruskin, an admirer of the Pre-Raphaelites, and a not undiscriminating judge of young poets and juvenilia in general, would encourage him to recite to her the compositions which were now germinating so fast and furious in his brain. He would proclaim these poems in the saloon at Wallington—standing on a chair, his body backwardly rigid, his voice rasping up to a note of vatic and falsetto ecstasy, his arms pressed rigidly to his side, his hands working upwards and downwards with stiff down-pointing fingers and with the extricating gestures of a man seeking to push himself up and out of some imprisoning quicksand. From time to time

with two fingers of his right hand he would slowly
close his left eyelid : a wholly unaccountable gesture.
All this with a complete absence of self-consciousness,
with a rigid intensity, which would produce upon his
auditors a sense not so much of the grotesque as of
something unbelievably inhuman, of something almost
unbearably strange.

The admiring sympathy, the prudent encouragement of Lady Trevelyan proved to Swinburne, during
this summer of 1858, a very welcome solace, a very
necessary tonic in what, but for her, would have been a
bitter period of disappointment. For in the preceding
spring he had again competed for the Newdigate and
had again been unsuccessful. The subject for that
year was " The Discovery of the North-West Passage ",
and the prize was awarded to a Mr. Latham of
Brasenose. Swinburne in after years would never
refer to this, his second failure to obtain the Newdigate,
and but for the rather pathetic chance that the Admiral
himself preserved the manuscript, neither the poem
itself nor the circumstances of its composition would
ever have been disclosed. It is not wholly surprising,
perhaps, that the examiners should not have accorded
the prize to Swinburne's poem. In the first place it
did not deal with the prescribed subject, but was
confined solely to the fate and adventures of Sir
John Franklin and his companions ; in the second
place it did not fulfil the conditions of the Newdigate
bequest, under which all compositions must be sub-
mitted in the form of rhymed couplets. It is quite
possible, therefore, that the poem was disqualified from
the outset on the grounds of its matter and its form,
and that the examiners did not feel themselves justified

in giving further attention to a composition which, upon
the face of it, fulfilled none of the requirements, and
had coped with none of the limitations, by which other
and less opinionated competitors had felt it their duty
to be bound.   On no other supposition can we explain
how the examiners, who after all were men of culture
fully alive to the responsibility of their ungrateful task,
could have failed to detect in Swinburne's " Death of
Sir John Franklin " not merely the technical purity and
formal elevation for which they were looking, but a
quivering note of personal experience, a note of personal
intensity, strong-winged and eager, seeking for escape.
For against the arctic background of his ordered
theme—

> Out in some barren creek of the cold seas,
> Where the slow shapes of the grey water-weed
> Freeze midway as the languid inlets freeze—

Swinburne has set this epic of endurance, giving a wider
significance to those dumb and dim explorers, investing
them with that faith and fire of adventurous patriotism
which had sent the Elizabethans out from little English
harbours across the uncharted seas.   His own love of
daring, his passion for the Elizabethans, had thus
inspired the poem with an afflatus stronger than that
of any mere mechanic exercise, and had given to it a
shape, a continuity, and a meaning which places it high
in the second rank of English patriotic verse.   The
dominant note, as is fitting for a subject thus conceived,
is Shakespearian ; it may be thought by some that at
moments this note is too decidedly reminiscent, too
obviously imitative ; such lines as

> There is no nobler word
> In the large writing and scored marge of time,

may perhaps savour sometimes of the *pastiche* ; but
what more noble echo of St. Crispin could be devised
than this prelude to the fifth section of his poem :

> What praise shall England give these men her friends ?
> For while the bays and the large channels flow,
> In the broad sea between the iron ends
> Of the poised world where no safe sail may be,
> And for white miles the hard ice never blends
> With the chill washing edges of dull sea . . .
> So long the record of these men shall stand,
> Because they chose not life but rather death,
> Each side being weighed with a most equal hand
> Because the gift they had of English breath
> They did give back to England for her sake,
> Like those dead seamen of Elizabeth
> And those who wrought with Nelson or with Blake
> To do great England service their lives long—
> High honour shall they have ; their deeds shall make
> Their spoken names sound sweeter than all song.

And with this Shakespearian exordium Swinburne
proceeds to recount the death of Sir John Franklin.
It is not to be supposed, however, that this admirable
poem is merely archaic in its tenor, or that it does not
contain notes of a more modern melody. There are,
for instance, a few tremulous passages in which vibrate
the feminine Pre-Raphaelite stress :

> Is this the end ? Is praise so light a thing
> As rumour unto rumour tendereth
> And time wears out of care and thanksgiving ?

And in the eighth section, when the explorers imprisoned in their circle of summer ice think back on
England on " the green fields or the May weather's
blue ", there is a sudden passage which is neither
Elizabethan in its quality nor yet Pre-Raphaelite, but
which strikes the first unmistakable note of *Poems and
Ballads* :

> New feet are in the waymarks of their feet,
> The bitter savour of remembered sweet
> No doubt did touch their lips in some sharp guise,
> No doubt the pain of thought and fever-heat
> Put Passion in the patience of their eyes.

There can be little doubt, therefore, that by the spring of 1858 Swinburne had found his voice : whether he at once exercised it in his own distinctive melodies is more questionable.   In the dedication of 1865 affixed to *Poems and Ballads* he speaks of the verses therein collected as being the fruit of seven years :

> Some scattered in seven years' traces
>   As they fell from the boy that was then ;
> Long left among idle green places,
>   Or gathered but now among men.

But, as I have said, Swinburne is not very reliable as his own bibliographer.   It is probable, indeed, that few if any of the *Poems and Ballads* date from before 1860, and that after composing the " Death of Franklin " Swinburne continued for two years to copy the works of other men, of Morris in *Queen Yseult*, of Shakespeare in the first seven of his unpublished Undergraduate Sonnets, of Rossetti in the eighth and last of that series.   We hear also of a dramatic lyric called " The Golden House ", and of an incomplete epic upon the Albigenses, both of which have disappeared.   Moreover, before the end of 1859 he had completed his first draft of *Rosamond*, which, though approved by William Morris, was shortly afterwards committed to the flames and rewritten.   Three other unpublished plays also belong to this period, composed in close imitation of the style of Beaumont and Fletcher, namely, *The Laws of Corinth*, finished in 1858 ; *Laugh and Lie Down*, an uncompleted farce, in close imitation of Fletcher's more unpleasing mannerisms; and *The Loyal Servant*, composed between 1859 and 1860. Such labours, inconclusive as they were, left him but little time in which to attend to his University studies. John Nichol had by then left Balliol, but the intemperate habits which Swinburne had already contracted led him into many excesses. Jowett became uneasy: he began to fear that the College authorities would be forced to take the strongest disciplinary measures— "Balliol thereby making itself as ridiculous as University had made itself about Shelley". He ordered Swinburne to retire for a season, and during the winter of 1859-60, and the succeeding spring and summer, the poet resided therefore with Dr. Stubbs at Navestock Vicarage in Essex. In October he returned to Oxford and lodged in Broad Street. Again he succumbed to drink and violence; his landlady complained: " I have had me fill ", she complained, " of these tiresome Balliol gentlemen ". And it was thus that at the end of 1860 Swinburne left Oxford without taking his degree.

" My Oxonian career ", he recorded later, " culminated in total and scandalous failure "; or again, " My connection with Oxford is something like Shelley's ". This was certainly an exaggeration: the authorities of Balliol had as usual been wisely tolerant; it was not against them that Swinburne's unfilial attitude was subsequently directed; it was against the University as a whole, against those anonymous examiners who had in two successive years rejected him for the Newdigate; for in this, predominantly, lay the acid gall of future recollections.

So when, in his seventy-first year, he received from

Lord Curzon the offer of an honorary degree, that so signal atonement proffered by the University in the person of her most distinguished Chancellor, Swinburne, with a somewhat graceless and embittered courtesy, refused.

CHAPTER IV

THE PRE-RAPHAELITE INTERLUDE, 1860–1865

ADMIRAL SWINBURNE was displeased by this abrupt conclusion to his son's career at Balliol : there was some correspondence on the subject, the exact purport of which is not recorded ; it is to be noted, however, that in the not dissimilar case of Reginald in *Love's Cross-currents*, Captain Harewood, the hero's father, wrote to his son as follows : " Absolute inert idleness and wilful vanity, after a long course of violated discipline, brought you in time to the dishonourable failure you had been at no pains to avoid ". The Admiral's own letters were perhaps less stilted than Captain Harewood's ; but there were unpleasant suggestions of a profession (Algernon had been studying law at Navestock), and a profession, now that he could be neither a lighthouse-keeper nor in the light dragoons, was a highly distasteful subject : so distasteful that Algernon did not return that winter to Bonchurch, but repaired to Capheaton and to the humorous hazel eyes of Lady Trevelyan. From this Northumberland retreat, and with the tactful intervention of his mother, the slight difference with the Admiral, a not unindulgent father, was repaired ; and after further negotiations Algernon was accorded an annual allowance, which eventually attained the then generous figure of £400, and informed that he might live how and where he pleased. By which prudent action the Admiral retained his love and confidence, and was able, in the coming years, to offer him a constant and very salutary haven from the tempests that so gratuitously followed.

It was thus in December 1860 that Swinburne first appeared in London, and established himself in rooms at 16 Grafton Street, Fitzroy Square. He lost no time in renewing relations with his Pre-Raphaelite friends, with Burne-Jones and William Morris, with Madox Brown in Fortress Terrace, and with Rossetti at 14 Chatham Place. The intellectual stimulus of 1857 did not recur ; and indeed these important years from 1860 to 1865 are strikingly eventless and unproductive. The experiences had been absorbed, but they were slow in germinating. In 1864 he composed a short morality play for insertion as an interlude in a book written by his cousin Mrs. Disney Leith under the pseudonym of " Mark Dennis ", and the title of *The Children in the Chapel*. In the same year he conceived the plan of a sequence of stories in the manner of Boccaccio, and actually published the first of this series in *Once a Week* and under the title of " Dead Love ". It is true also that during these four years he actually composed some of the more important poems and ballads which were published in 1866, that " Laus Veneris ", " Faustine ", " The Sundew ", and " The Triumph of Time " date from about 1862, the " Hermaphroditus " from 1863, and " Itylus " and " Félise " from 1864. Moreover, throughout the latter year he was intent on the composition of *Atalanta*. But when we consider the amazing rapidity with which he wrote his lyrical poems, and the constant stimulus which he received from a circle of intellectual friends lavish in their mutual admiration, it becomes indeed strange that he should have waited till his twenty-ninth year before publishing anything of serious importance ; it becomes, indeed, pathetic to compare the amazing fecundity of his production between 1880 and 1886 with the tenuous yield of his adolescence, the comparative silence of his April and his May. The explanation of this phenomenon is not, I think, to be found in his mode of life, which was not in those years any more eccentric or self-indulgent than in the comparatively productive period between 1865 and 1879. Nor is it to be attributed to idleness, certainly not to indifference, only partially to an excessive indulgence in conversation. These symptoms were the effects rather than the causes of his unproductiveness. The real reason lies, I think, in the fact that Swinburne was unconsciously disconcerted by his own incapacity to accept further experiences ; and that while hesitating for a time to draw upon the experiences of his childhood and puberty, he sought in vain to place himself in a sensitive relation to something new. In other words, although by 1858 he had found his voice, he did not till 1864 find himself. He tended in the interval to replace his imperviousness to impressions, by exploiting his accessibility to influences ; and this process led him inevitably to draw from literature the stimulus that he could not readily obtain from life. His obsession by the Elizabethan drama, his more recent admiration for Browning, thus diverted his energies from lyrical poetry at the very period when lyrical poetry should have been the fittest communication of his experience. His admiration for Rossetti, the predominant Pre-Raphaelite atmosphere in which he lived, obscured for a while those boyhood impressions which were his only organised experiences, while his fatal facility for imitation made it all too easy for him to write verses in the manner of Morris or of Rossetti—verses which he could scarcely claim, or feel, to be his own. It is significant that in such circumstances he should have turned his mind in other directions—in the direction of fiction, in which, until George Meredith appeared on the scene, he essayed to dabble, and predominantly in the direction of poetical drama. From the outset, however, his enthusiasm for the latter form of self-expression received a serious check : in December 1860 he published with Moxon his two undergraduate dramas of *The Queen Mother* and *Rosamond*. They attracted no attention either unfavourable or the reverse : they were simply ignored. " Of all stillborn books," Swinburne remarked afterwards to Sir Edmund Gosse, " *The Queen Mother* was the stillest." Sir Edmund Gosse himself attributes this lack of public interest to the unfamiliarity of the models " on which the apparatus of the drama was formed ". Swinburne had set out deliberately to reproduce the manner of Chapman's French tragedies, of the *Tragedy of Chabot* and the two plays on Bussy d'Ambois ; he was also much influenced at the time by the *Joseph and his Brethren* of Charles J. Wells, a forgotten drama of 1824 which Rossetti had pronounced to be " stunning ", and from which Swinburne in his turn had received one of the most inexplicable of his recurrent " shocks of adoration ". But there are other causes which blinded the critics to the very real interest and originality of *The Queen Mother*.

The construction of the play is throughout somewhat turgid, the central theme is continually being obscured by purely derivative digressions, and the minor characters—Yolande, Guise, La Rochefoucauld, Brantôme—are out of proportion to their intrinsic value in the composition. This lack of line and perspective was a fault which Swinburne was never enabled entirely to outlive, even as he remained throughout his life devoid of any sense of audience, of any realisation that what he himself knew or understood might to his readers be either unknown or obscure. The critics of 1860 may also have been disconcerted by the blatant Elizabethanism of some of the more rhetorical passages, by lines like—

> And the hard pulse of his outlaboured hour,

or

> Each his own loathing and particular sore,

or by the too obvious Shakespearianism of—

> Or now, this gold that makes me up a king,
> This apprehensive note and mark of time,
> This token'd kingdom, this well-tested worth
> Wherein my brows exalt and are begirt.

Nor can they have relished the admixture with these early seventeenth-century brocades of what to them was the broadcloth of Browning, of such foreshortened verse as—

> I would I were clear of you.
> What would you get ?   You are a great queen, grave soul,
> Crown-shaped i' the head ; your work is wonderful
> And stoops me to you by the neck, but I
> Can scantly read it out.

They may also have been slightly dismayed by the recurrence throughout the drama of that tremulous and wistful chord, that haunting vibration, that note of unappeased yearning which they could not but recognise and condemn as the motif of the Pre-Raphaelite movement, the insidious poison of which was already infecting the simpler sweethearting of mid-Victorian England :

> Nay, I shall try your trust. Sit by me, so ;
> Lay your hands thus. By God, how fair you are.
> It does amaze me ; surely God felt glad
> The day he finished making you. Eh, sweet,
> You have the eyes men choose to paint, you know ;
> And just that soft turn in the little throat
> And bluish colour in the lower lid . . .

It is little wonder that, thus disconcerted, they should not have realised the dramatic qualities, the vivid characterisation of the play itself, or the magnificent blank-verse passages, the skilful French and English lyrics which it contains. Our own interest in *The Queen Mother* is aroused not so much by the story itself ; not even by the several character scenes such as the dialogues between Charles IX. and Catherine de' Medici, or the curious interview by the bedside of the wounded Coligny ; not even so much by the magnificent torch-lit finale of the Massacre of St. Bartholomew, as by those passages in which we recognise the original note of Swinburne, in which one can trace the threads of independent treatment. The purely imitative defects of *The Queen Mother* have already been indicated : it is in the aspect given to love, in the character of Denise, that the peculiar and specialised quality of Swinburne's experience can first be recognised. For in both these respects *The Queen Mother* is the precursor of *Atalanta*. The essence of the Pre-Raphaelite treatment of love was that of tremulous and mystic longing for the unattained ; it reflected the mediaeval theory of sensuous but selfless service. This formula was not, except superficially, accepted by Swinburne : with him love became less spiritual, and in an important sense less real ; for him the love-contrast between joy and suffering, the bitter-sweet on which he delighted to dwell, was born in the actual moment of attainment. The peculiar immaturity, not to say unreality, of his own sexual experience too often tempted him to diverge upon the tangent of sadism ; but in its less physical form, or more accurately in the reaction produced by this same cruelty of lust, the acute tension between revolt and submission formed the basic inspiration of some of his finest and most original lyrics. It would indeed be no exaggeration to contend that the most original poetic quality of Swinburne was his especial sensitiveness to this particular tension— whether conceived in the form of that between pain and pleasure, between cruelty and sacrifice, between hate and adoration, or between mutiny and obedience. All these elements, the worst and the best, are present in *The Queen Mother*. On the one hand we have such lines as—

> And I now pluck the finished fruit of it
> Planted by bitter touches of the lip;
> False breath, hot vows, the broken speech of lust,
> By finger pinches and keen mouths that bite
> Their hard kiss through.

And on the other hand we have the character of Denise, " A white long woman with thick hair ", an Artemis of the Court of France, a girl frightened by the cruelty of love, a clear white virginal flame—the precursor of Atalanta.

These qualities and these defects are equally apparent
in the shorter play of *Rosamond*, which possesses at
least the advantage of dealing with a central and
localised episode, and of thus avoiding all undue wealth
of historical material, in which Swinburne, who was
more of a scholar than a playwright, was always apt to
flounder and to lose his way.   For the main action of
the drama takes place in Rosamond's bower, the theme
is love only and the hate produced by love, and the
form as compared with *The Queen Mother* is predominantly lyrical.   Rosamond is represented as a
trapped and gentle figure, glorying at moments in her
concubinage, conscious that she has become thereby
one of the eternal figures of romance :

> Yea, I am found the woman in all tales,
> The face caught always in the story's face :
> I Helen, holding Paris by the lips,
> Smote Hector through the head : I Cressida
> So kissed men's mouths that they went sick or mad,
> Stung right at brain with me ; I Guenevere
> Made my queen's eyes so precious and my hair
> Delicate with such gold in its soft ways
> And my mouth honied so for Launcelot, . . .

and with it all, a little frightened :

> Fear is the cushion for the feet of love
> Painted with colours for his ease-taking ;

and at moments a little dismayed by :

> Sick words and sorrowful
> Of love's hard sweet and hunger of harsh hours.

This variation between fear and triumph, between joy
and despair, between revolt and submission, reaches
its climax in the beautiful dialogue between King
Henry and Rosamond, which is preluded and closed
by the pulsation of a French lyric, and accompanied

F

throughout by the soft patter of the rain-drops upon the limes. Nor is it conceivable how this scene, at least, should have escaped the attention, or even the hostility, of contemporary criticism.

The failure of his two published dramas increased in Swinburne the mood of discouragement and inertia which, as has already been indicated, lasted from 1860 to 1864. Of his external life during this inactive period there is but little to record. His grandfather died in September 1860, and the winter of that year was spent with his parents at Mentone, from which sojourn he derived only an abiding hatred for the Mediterranean in general and the Côte d'Azur in particular. " That salt lake " he would call it, and thereafter the Riviera became for him that " frousy fringe of a blue pond ". From there he paid his first visit to Italy, travelling *via* Genoa and Turin to Milan and Venice. In the spring of 1861 he returned to London, resuming his worship of Rossetti, and confirming into terms of " high facetious familiarity " the friendship which he had already formed with Lord Houghton, that paragon of literary impresarios. The year 1862 was marked by two unfortunate events. On February 10 Swinburne dined at the Sablonnière Hotel in Leicester Square with Rossetti and his wife, the enigmatic Lizzie Siddal. Rossetti saw the latter home after the dinner, went out again to the Working-Men's College, and returned to find her lying dead with an empty bottle of laudanum at her side. Swinburne was obliged to give evidence at the inquest ; he was bitterly distressed ; he promised to keep Rossetti and his brother company in their loneliness. It was agreed that they should keep house together, and by the autumn of that year Swinburne, after a temporary sojourn at 77 Newman Street, Oxford Street, moved into Tudor House at 16 Cheyne Walk. This was not a successful undertaking. Rossetti, it is true, was tolerant, if somewhat patronising, of his " little Northumbrian friend " ; nor was William Michael anything but friendly and kind. But a room had also been reserved for George Meredith, and upon the nerves of Meredith, Gabriel's " little Northumbrian friend " grated considerably. So that the experiment was not of very continuous or protracted duration.

The year 1862 was also marked for Swinburne by an exceedingly distressing occurrence : he fell in love. The object of this his sole infatuation was, as Sir Edmund Gosse relates, a " graceful and vivacious girl ", the daughter of Dr., afterwards Sir John Simon, the friend of Ruskin and Burne-Jones. It appears that this young lady had treated Swinburne with particular kindness. " She gave him roses," writes Sir Edmund Gosse, " she played and sang to him, and he conceived from her gracious ways an encouragement which she was far from seriously intending." Swinburne proposed. The suddenness, and no doubt the hysterical violence of this declaration took her entirely by surprise; she laughed in his face. And it is to so unhappy an incident that we owe " The Triumph of Time ", the most enduring of all Swinburne's single lyrics.

Smarting under the lash of that cruel discomfiture, he escaped to Northumberland. In a few weeks he drifted back to London, where he discovered on a cheap bookstall a discarded copy of FitzGerald's *Omar Khayyám*. Waving the book above his flaming head he fluttered into Meredith's cottage at Copsham, and that afternoon, with the music of the quatrains in his brain, he wrote the " Laus Veneris " while dancing like a scarlet leaf on Copsham Mound. The summer found him staying with Lord Houghton at Fryston, as the fellow-guest of Thackeray and his two daughters, and in March 1863 he proceeded to Paris, making the acquaintance of Whistler and of Fantin Latour, frequenting the studios and the Louvre, writing his poem to the recumbent figure of Hermaphroditus. His constitution, which till then, in spite of his deficient neural equilibrium, had been almost robust, began at this date to twitch under the strain of alcoholic excess, and it is from the spring of 1863 that date the first symptoms of those strange epileptiform seizures which from now on caused his friends such continuous embarrassment and such acute anxiety. He proceeded for the summer to Tintagel, and for the autumn to the Isle of Wight ; his health, as always after a climax of fits and drinking, was rapidly re-established ; his mode of life, for the period of these seaside sojourns, became more regular ; he embarked on the composition of *Atalanta*.

In February 1864 he joined his family in Italy. Within a few weeks he left them, and proceeded alone to Florence. It was not as a tourist that he journeyed, but as a pilgrim. Armed with his own reverence, and a letter of introduction from Lord Houghton, he had come to lay the worship of his twenty-six years at the feet of his supreme hero : he was about to visit Walter Savage Landor at No. 93 Via della Chiesa :

> I came as one whose thoughts half linger,
>   Half run before ;
> The youngest to the oldest singer
>   That England bore.

The hero-worship of Swinburne was no passing phase of boyhood; it was a deep and persistent religion, and the most potent of his incantations was ever " Let us now praise famous men ". Of all his experiences this at least never failed to stimulate a response : nor was there any direction in which his constant preoccupation with the conflict between the muscular and the flaccid, the violent and the submissive, found an easier vent. " I am not sure ", he wrote, " that any other emotion is so durable and persistently delicious as that of worship, when your God is indubitable and incarnate before your eyes." Or again, and this time in the person of Reginald Harewood : " I feel my betters in my blood : they send a heat and sting all through one at first sight. And the delight of feeling small and giving in when one does get sight of them is beyond words." It was in such a mood, therefore, that Swinburne on the 3rd of March, having sent his letter in advance, approached the Via della Chiesa, quivering in anticipation of the expected " shock of adoration ". Landor, for his part, was not equally prepared for the occasion. In the first place he was eighty-nine years old and by nature hardly tractable ; and in the second place he was not himself very addicted to " shocks of adoration ", had himself never met anybody " in whose presence he felt inferiority, excepting Kosciusco ". The sudden irruption, therefore, of this small red-headed stranger, his genuflexions, his hysterical hand-kissing and his flood of high-pitched ululation, seriously perturbed the leonine old gentleman, left him speechless and embarrassed ; the visitor was asked to leave at once. " I found him," Swinburne wrote to Lord Houghton, " owing I suspect to the violent weather, too much weakened and confused to realise the fact of the introduction without distress. In effect he seemed so feeble and incompatible that I came away in a grievous state of disappointment and depression myself, fearing I was really too late. But taking heart of grace I wrote him a line of apology and explanation. . . . " This apology produced forgiveness and a further invitation : the second interview was more successful ; they conversed at length and calmly ; on his departure Swinburne was presented by force with a sham Correggio. " My grandfather ", he wrote again to Lord Houghton, " was upon the whole *mieux conservé* ; but he had written no Hellenics."

It was during his stay in Florence that Swinburne wrote " Itylus ", in a high-walled garden at Fiesole, deafened by noonday nightingales ; and from there he proceeded over the Tuscan hills to San Gimignano and Siena. The summer found him back in England staying with Jowett at Kynance Cove, completing *Atalanta* and composing, with Jowett's wholly indispensable assistance, the portentous Greek verses in which that poem is dedicated to Landor. In the autumn he returned in a nervous and intractable mood to Cheyne Walk. He would dance about Rossetti's studio " like a wild cat " : his temperamental lack of sympathy with Meredith led to many an outburst— and the voice of Algernon would rasp up into high-pitched outbursts of childish rage, turning the easy disorder of Tudor House into pandemonium. Rossetti irritated Swinburne as he irritated Meredith by his hearty appetite at breakfast ; Swinburne annoyed Meredith by his " damned nut-cracker epigrams " and by his inveterate habit of sliding down the banisters and arriving with a flump on the ground floor. It was indeed fortunate that Ruskin had abandoned his early intention of himself joining the establishment. This joint existence had in any case become impossible ; and one day Swinburne mildly and with docile courtesy took his departure, staying for a while in Mount Street, and then establishing himself at 22A Dorset Street, where he remained four years.

In his biography of the poet Sir Edmund Gosse has drawn attention to the curious circumstance that until Swinburne was in his twenty-sixth year he had no opportunity of reaching a public wider than his own private friends. Within the then narrow circle of the Pre-Raphaelites the poems that he had composed between 1859 and 1862 were widely known and enthusiastically acclaimed. It was not, however, till the year 1862 that he was introduced by Lord Houghton to Richard Holt Hutton, part-editor and part-proprietor of the *Spectator*. At Hutton's invitation he furnished, for publication in that journal, certain of his more recent poems, and between April and September 1862 the *Spectator* in this way published no less than seven of Swinburne's lyrics, namely, " Before Parting ", " A Song in Time of Order", "After Death", "A Song in Time of Revolution ", " August ", " Faustine ", and " The Sundew ". To the same paper he contributed a letter defending Meredith's " Modern Love ", as well as two unsigned articles on *Les Misérables* and on Baudelaire's *Fleurs du Mal* which, after its suppression in 1857, had been republished in 1861. Copies of these articles were sent by Swinburne to Victor Hugo and Baudelaire respectively : the former replied with his usual lavish encomium, thereby confirming into a monomania the then merely formal worship of Swinburne; Baudelaire's reply, owing to an oversight, never reached London. And by the autumn of 1862 Swinburne quarrelled with Hutton, and did not again appear before the public till April 1865.

For it was at that date that he published *Atalanta*.

CHAPTER V

" ATALANTA IN CALYDON ", 1865

THE experiences which fuse in this, the most interesting of all Swinburne's works, were of a diverse nature. It has already been suggested that he was not, in the exact sense of the term, an outstanding classical scholar; but his knowledge of the Greek stage, his particular knowledge of Sophocles and Aeschylus, his faculty of memorising and reciting whole choruses and passages of his favourite plays, had already placed him in a very sensitive relation towards the atmosphere and the harmonics of the Greek drama. The bright white light of the Attic spirit came to him therefore as no new or fortuitous illumination, and it was almost with deliberation, certainly with relief, that he turned from the distracting influence of the Pre-Raphaelites to a theme in which his more direct, because earlier, experience could find an outlet.

There exists no evidence to show by what chances Swinburne was guided to the tale of Atalanta. The story of the wrath of Artemis against the men of Calydon is indeed referred to in the ninth book of the *Iliad*, but we find no mention therein of the virgin Atalanta, the Homeric story representing Meleager as already married to the fair-girdled Kleopatra. Nor is it to be supposed that the theme was suggested either by Apollodorus or by the Euripidean fragment on Meleager. One may conjecture perhaps that the bright, light name of Atalanta first attracted his attention in the obscure reference to " Atalanta's better part " which occurs in *As You Like It*, and that this led him *via* the Classical Dictionary to the metamorphosis of Ovid —a poet who would not, in ordinary circumstances, have provided any inspiration. Be this as it may, the very condensation of the legend, the clear-cut conflict which it provides between predestination and free-will, between revolt and submission, renders it eminently suitable for treatment in the Old Greek manner. The argument is in itself a simple one, and is summarised by Swinburne in a short foreword couched in curiously archaic language. Oeneus, king of Calydon, had offended Artemis by omitting her from his rituals, and she retaliated, first by organising war and invasion, and then by sending a boar to lay waste the crops of Aetolia. An expedition was organised to slay the boar, and among the volunteers arrived Atalanta, the Arcadian virgin, herself beloved of Artemis. Meleager, a young veteran of the Golden Fleece, the son of Oeneus and his wife Althaea, falls in love with the virgin Atalanta, to whom, when the boar is slain, he presents the spoils. Toxeus and Plexippus, brothers of Queen Althaea, resent his action, and in their attempts to snatch the booty from Atalanta they are both killed by their nephew Meleager. Althaea, at the time of Meleager's birth, had been warned by the Fates that he would live only so long as the brand in the fire before her remained unconsumed ; she had plucked this brand from the flames and guarded it in her bosom as the symbol of her son's existence.

When, therefore, she hears of the murder of her two brothers, she plunges the brand again into the flames, and as it whitens into ashes the body of Meleager is itself consumed. " And his mother ", concludes Swinburne's argument, " also endured not long after for very sorrow ; and this was the end, and the end of that hunting."

The manner in which Swinburne has expanded this fable into the forms of a Greek drama merits more detailed analysis. The play is divided, as we should say, into two acts, the first consisting of a prelude and three scenes culminating in the departure of Meleager and Atalanta for the hunt ; the second, which has four scenes and a short epilogue, giving the solution of the tragedy. The intervals, or " curtains ", are provided by choric odes of varying length and import. More technically the scheme of the drama may be summarised as follows :

    I. *Prologue*. Spoken by Chief Huntsman.
   II. *Parodos*. " When the hounds of Spring . . ."
  III. *Episode I*. Althaea tells the story of the boar, and the story of Meleager's birth ; she speaks of the coming of Atalanta, and of her son's passion, as the final revenge of Artemis, and inveighs against the implacability of the gods.
  IV. *Stasimon I*. Chorus : " Before the beginning of years ".
  V. *Episode II*. Meleager and his mother : dialogue on the conflict between love and duty.
  VI. *Stasimon II*. Chorus : " We have seen thee, Oh Love " ; Hymn to Venus Anadyomene.
 VII. *Episode III*. Atalanta, Toxeus and Plexippus enter. Departure for the hunt.
VIII. *Stasimon III*. Chorus : " Who have given men speech " ; Revolt against the gods.
  IX. *Episode IV*. Herald announces the death of the boar.

Such was the scheme, of almost Phidian symmetry, within the limits of which Swinburne proposed to tell the tale of the " most fair and fearful " Atalanta. The skill with which he constructed his symphony can be apprehended only by a complete and uninterrupted reading of the play itself. It will be well, however, to trace the development which he has given to the drama and to indicate some of the more characteristic passages.

The scene is set upon some terrace-bastion of the palace looking out over the ravaged plains of Calydon to the Aetolian mountains, where lurks the violent beast, symbol of the wrath of Artemis. In the Court below have already gathered the heroes and the hunters of Greece, waiting for the sunrise; as a faint undertone, throughout the opening movement of the play, rumbles the dust and murmur of their gathering. The Chief Huntsman, solitary in the half-light before the dawn, advances with an invocation to Aurora, " maiden and mistress of the months and stars ", his voice rising with the slowly increasing light into a prayer to Apollo, and an appeal to Artemis.

With the concluding lines of the Prologue the Chorus of fifteen Aetolian virgins advance slowly for the parodos, bearing wreaths of flowers for the altar of Artemis, and as the Chief Huntsman closes his monologue, they slide gently into the famous processional anapaests, pacing the rhythmic movement of the emmeleia while the dawn breaks slowly over Calydon :

> When the hounds of spring are on winter's traces,
>   The mother of months in meadow or plain
> Fills the shadows and windy places
>   With lisp of leaves and ripples of rain ;
> And the brown bright nightingale amorous
> Is half assuaged for Itylus,
> For the Thracian ships and the foreign faces,
>   The tongueless vigil, and all the pain. . . .

With the fourth stanza of the Chorus the melody shifts suddenly into the minor key, closing with an ode to spring and dying away in soft pulsating notes of love and youth and sunshine. It is with something of a shock, with the jarring contrast of reality, that Althaea (the sole really tragic figure in what, but for her, would be a choral entertainment if not a Theocritean pastoral) enters already fierce and flaming as befits one chosen as the tool of divine vengeance. A sharp duologue or stichomythia follows :

ALTHAEA. Look ye say well, and know not what ye say :
          For all my sleep is turned into a fire,
          And all my dreams to stuff that kindles it.
CHORUS. Yet one doth well being patient of the gods.
ALTHAEA. Yea, lest they smite us with some four-foot plague.
CHORUS. But when time spreads find out some herb for it.
ALTHAEA. And with their healing herbs infect our blood.

Althaea then embarks upon her plaint against the implacable cruelty of Artemis, who has now afflicted Meleager with love for Atalanta. The passage is an admirable adaptation of the Greek manner to a matter which is essentially un-Hellenic in conception :

ALTHAEA. Yea, but a curse she hath sent above all these
To hurt us where she healed us ; and hath lit
Fire where the old fire went out, and where the wind
Slackened, hath blown on us with deadlier air.
CHORUS. What storm is this that tightens all our sail ?
ALTHAEA. Love, a thwart sea-wind full of rain and foam.
CHORUS. Whence blown, and born under what stormier star ?
ALTHAEA. Southward across Euenus from the sea.
CHORUS. Thy speech turns toward Arcadia like blown wind.
ALTHAEA. Sharp as the north sets when the snows are out.
CHORUS. Nay, for this maiden hath no touch of love. . . .

Having stated the complication of the tragedy, Althaea proceeds to indicate its solution and to narrate the mystery of Meleager's birth, the secret of the brand, concluding with a note of pessimism, a little note of helpless resignation.

In the third Chorus, which follows immediately on the plaint of Althaea, the reaction against the intolerable cruelty of the gods in having mingled pain with pleasure, in having fouled the springs of life with the poison of death, is echoed and summarised with gentle resignation :

Before the beginning of years
There came to the making of man
Time, with a gift of tears ;
Grief, with a glass that ran ;
Pleasure, with pain for leaven ;
Summer, with flowers that fell ;
Remembrance fallen from heaven,
And madness risen from hell ;

> Strength without hands to smite ;
>   Love that endures for a breath ;
> Night, the shadow of light,
>   And life, the shadow of death.
>
> They gave him light in his ways,
>   And love, and a space for delight,
> And beauty and length of days,
>   And night, and sleep in the night.
> His speech is a burning fire ;
>   With his lips he travaileth ;
> In his heart is a blind desire,
>   In his eyes foreknowledge of death ;
> He weaves, and is clothed with derision ;
>   Sows, and he shall not reap ;
> His life is a watch or a vision
>   Between a sleep and a sleep.

These clouded litanies are broken suddenly by the entry of the young and shining Meleager, by the re-introduction of the *motif* of youth and love and life :

> Oh, sweet new heaven and air without a star,

he cries, and it is with the zest of young adventure that he names for his mother the heroes gathered in the court below. It is not long, however, before the *motif* of death and tragedy begins to weave its sullen harmonies through this triumphant catalogue ; for the mention of her brothers Toxeus and the " violent-souled " Plexippus reawakens in Althaea the pang of her presentiment, and she essays to warn her son against the menace of his strange un-sexed Arcadian virgin, pleading with him the virtues of abnegation and the rewards of self-control. He answers that he is no child to fall an easy prey to danger and temptation ; has he not sailed

> Clear through the irremeable Symplegades ?

has he not known " Medea, deadlier than the sea " ?

Nor is his present passion the mere mortal weakness of a boy in love ; it is not love but worship that he feels for Atalanta :

> Most fair and fearful, feminine, a god,
> Faultless ; whom I that love not, being unlike,
> Fear, and give honour, and choose from all the gods.

At this stage Oeneus, the type of common reason, endeavours to conciliate their differences, but Althaea persists, founding her final appeal on the claims of motherhood, on her memories of Meleager when he was a child. Meleager is left disturbed and uncertain while the Chorus break into their " Curse of Venus " with its famous anapaestic opening :

We have seen thee, O Love, thou art fair ; thou art goodly, O Love ;
Thy wings make light in the air as the wings of a dove.
Thy feet are as winds that divide the stream of the sea ;
Earth is thy covering to hide thee, the garment of thee.
Thou art swift and subtle and blind as a flame of fire ;
Before thee the laughter, behind thee the tears of desire.

It is at the end of this long choric ode to Venus Anadyomene that Atalanta makes her entry. The day has now risen from above the hills, and in her first words she greets the Sun. Bright and virginal she enters, her bow and quiver swing lightly from her shoulders ; there are no sandals on her " natural, Greek and silver feet " ; she salutes her protector Artemis, a little fearful, for all her armed virginity, of the rough hunters who have gathered around her for the chase. Meleager reassures her :

> For thy name's sake and awe toward thy chaste head,
> O holiest Atalanta, no man dares
> Praise thee, though fairer than whom all men praise,
> And godlike for thy grace of hallowed hair

And holy habit of thine eyes, and feet
That make the blown foam neither swift nor white
Though the wind winnow and whirl it ; yet we praise
Gods, found because of thee adorable
And for thy sake praiseworthiest from all men :
Thee therefore we praise also, thee as these,
Pure, and a light lit at the hands of gods.

Meleager's intervention in favour of the Arcadian
Virgin occasions a rebuke from his two uncles Toxeus
and Plexippus, leading, through a short passage of
duologue, to a brazen clash and counter-clash of anger
and the climax of the first section of the drama.   The
transition from the complication to the solution, from
the creation of the problem to its catastrophic loosening,
is marked by a long choric diatribe against fate, against
the " bubbling bitterness of life and death ", culminating in a fierce denunciation of God :

None hath beheld him, none
Seen above other gods and shapes of things,
Swift without feet and flying without wings,
Intolerable, not clad with death or life,
    Insatiable, not known of night or day,
The lord of love and loathing and of strife
    Who gives a star and takes a sun away ;
Who shapes the soul, and makes her a barren wife
    To the earthly body and grievous growth of clay ;
Who turns the large limbs to a little flame
    And binds the great sea with a little sand ;
Who makes desire, and slays desire with shame ;
    Who shakes the heaven as ashes in his hand ;
Who, seeing the light and shadow for the same,
    Bids day waste night as fire devours a brand,
Smites without sword, and scourges without rod :
    The supreme evil, God.

This diatribe is incongruous, of course, not only
because it is out of keeping with the traditional rôle of
the Chorus, but also because it bears no relation to
what, at that central stage of the drama, any of the

G

participants would have actually been feeling. Fear, anxiety, apprehension are all that the dark prophecies and wailings of Althaea could by then have aroused in the breasts of the Aetolian virgins : if angered despair were to break from them, it should have come not immediately before, but during or after the main catastrophe. Placed as it is in a pause between the two main divisions of the action, it strikes too forcible a note for such an interlude, and by thus breaking for an instant the symphonic unity of the piece gives one a sudden picture of the fiery head and strident voice of Swinburne irrupting with FitzGerald philosophy and Balliol republicanism into the ordered and serene stasima of his own creation. That he was faintly aware of this himself can be deduced from the subtle gradation by which this central Chorus, after thus culminating in a blare of defiance, is toned into the minor key, dying away in fainter and fainter echoes and recurrences of anger, to subside finally in the soft clear chords of the conclusion.

To the echo of such submissiveness the second section of the play, the solution proper, is opened by the entry of a Herald to announce the slaying of the boar. A fine epic passage follows in which we are told of how the boar, first wounded by the arrow of Atalanta, was finally despatched in close combat by Meleager, and how thereat the Herald has sped to bring the joyful news to Calydon, leaving the huntsmen to flay the carcass and to divide the spoils. The Chorus breaks at once into a trochaic hymn to Artemis, a gentle tremolo as if to the sound of flutes, snapped suddenly by the entry of a Messenger, and with him a procession carrying on branches the covered corpses of Toxeus and Plexippus. A short duologue follows in which Meleager's murder of his uncles is broken to the distraught Althaea, and the Messenger then proceeds to recount in detail the quarrel which arose over the sharing of the spoil.

It is at this stage that arises the essential difficulty of combining in one drama the conceptions of the ancients with the sensibilities of to-day. Hitherto Swinburne had been able to retain the form and atmosphere of a Greek play without losing the attention or sympathy of a modern audience ; but with the realisation on the part of Althaea that her own son is the murderer of his uncles we come to the parting of the ways. Swinburne wisely rejects all endeavour to treat the conflict which then arises in Althaea as a problem of modern psychology. He makes Althaea the blind and maddened instrument of fate, " a blast of the envy of God ", the refinement of the cruelty of Artemis, who, while allowing the virgin Atalanta to slay the boar, was yet determined that this deliverance should entail an even greater misery on Calydon. The half-maddened speeches which the poet places in the burning mouth of Althaea are not intended as sophisms to explain and justify to the audience the impending blood-sacrifice of her son ; they are intended merely to show her as a helpless human victim, impelled by some supernatural evil, seeking at once to stimulate and justify herself in the deed which she is being forced, by some blind and cruel power, to perform. She thus, in frenzied deliberation, evokes for herself her childhood's love for her brothers, the need of vengeance, her own fierce hatred for that calm white virgin, " adorable, detestable ", who has brought this evil to the house.

In vain the Chorus remind her of other human ties and duties ; she replies to them with the old sophism of Antigone :

> For all things else and all men may renew ;
> Yea, son for son the gods may give and take,
> But never a brother or sister any more ;

and thus with a wail of fury she passes into the house to burn the brand on which depends the life of Meleager. After a short chorus on the suddenness of fate Althaea returns ; the deed has been accomplished ; gradually the divine madness leaves her, gradually there dawns upon her the realisation of what she has done :

CHORUS. I see a faint fire lightening from the hall.
ALTHAEA. Gaze, stretch your eyes, strain till the lids drop off.
CHORUS. Flushed pillars down the flickering vestibule.
ALTHAEA. Stretch with your necks like birds : cry, chirp as they.
CHORUS. And a long brand that blackens : and white dust.
ALTHAEA. O children, what is this ye see ? Your eyes
Are blinder than night's face at fall of moon.
That is my son, my flesh, my fruit of life.
My travail, and the year's weight of my womb.
Meleager, a fire enkindled of mine hands
And of mine hands extinguished ; this is he.
CHORUS. O gods, what word has flown out at thy mouth ?
ALTHAEA. I did this and I say this and I die.

Then with one final cry of agony, " O child, child, what have we made each other ? " Althaea veils herself in silence. She does not leave the stage : she remains there mute and pitiful throughout the coming threnodies, receiving in silent anguish the final forgiveness of Meleager.

The last speech of Althaea is followed by a Semichorus in which, panting and in tears, the Aetolian Virgins repeat to each other across the orchestra the horror of Althaea's deed :

SEMICHORUS.

She has filled with sighing the city,
    And the ways thereof with tears ;
She arose, she girdled her sides,
She set her face as a bride's ;
She wept, and she had no pity ;
    Trembled and felt no fears.

Her eyes were clear as the sun,
    Her brows were fresh as the day ;
She girdled herself with gold,
Her robes were manifold ;
But the days of her worship are done,
    Her praise is taken away.

For she set her hand to the fire,
    With her mouth she kindled the same :
As the mouth of a flute-player,
So was the mouth of her ;
With the might of her strong desire
    She blew the breath of the flame.

She set her hand to the wood,
    She took the fire in her hand ;
As one who is nigh to death,
She panted with strange breath ;
She opened her lips unto blood,
    She breathed and kindled the brand.

From the conclusion of this Semichorus to the end
of the play the treatment is, with the exception of
Meleager's farewell speech or exodos, exclusively
musical and rhythmic. The Second Messenger, who
now enters to prepare the audience for the coming of
the dying Meleager, indulges in no epic narrative or
extended monologue : his statements are rigid and
symmetrical, limited to three lines at a time of comparatively formal iambics, each statement matched by
a similarly balanced interjection on the part of the
Chorus. This fine melic passage is but the preparation
for the final Kommos, the most memorable and
exquisitely symphonic achievement of all Swinburne's

poetry. For, indeed, in re-reading that superb finale one realises how impossible it is to convey the impression of *Atalanta* by any formal analysis or any selected quotation : the effect should be cumulative and organic, each part is dependent on the whole, and in the final Kommos the harmonies and rhythms which have crossed and recrossed each other in a subtle interchange throughout the poem are gathered together in one vast symphonic summary, and the whole purport and beauty of the drama is disclosed.

I shall quote merely the two opening bars, and shall begin, somewhat arbitrarily, with the conclusion of the previous melic dialogue between the Second Messenger and the Chorus, in order to indicate the amazing subtlety of the transition into the Kommos proper, the sudden shifting into the minor key with the entry of Meleager. To understand the tension between horror and pity which is at this point evoked it is necessary to visualise, as Swinburne obviously visualised, the actual scenic and rhythmic effect of this culmination : the solitary figure of the Messenger upon the narrow isolated platform of the stage ; the fifteen Aetolian maidens responding dishevelled and almost maenad to his narration with conventionalised and simultaneous pantomime, or breaking with their Semichorus into breathless and shambling interjections ; the sudden change of time and movement on the entry of the dying Meleager ; the crescendo of dignity, the swaying symmetry of the lament which follows :

SECOND MESSENGER.

O son, he said, son, lift thine eyes, draw breath,
Pity me ; but Meleager with sharp lips
Gasped, and his face waxed like as sunburnt grass.

SEMICHORUS.

Cry aloud, O thou kingdom, O nation,
   O stricken, a ruinous land.

SECOND MESSENGER.

Whereat King Oeneus, straightening feeble knees,
With feeble hands heaved up a lessening weight,
And laid him sadly in strange hands, and wept.

SEMICHORUS.

Thou art smitten, her lord, her desire,
   Thy dear blood wasted as rain.

SECOND MESSENGER.

And they with tears and rendings of the beard
Bear hither a breathing body, wept upon
And lightening at each footfall, sick to death.

SEMICHORUS.

Thou madest thy sword as a fire,
   With fire for a sword thou art slain.

SECOND MESSENGER.

And lo, the feast turned funeral, and the crowns
Fallen ; and the huntress and the hunter trapped ;
And weeping and changed faces and veiled hair.

MELEAGER.

Let your hands meet
   Round the weight of my head ;
Lift ye my feet
   As the feet of the dead ;
For the flesh of my body is molten, the limbs of it molten
   as lead.

CHORUS.

O thy luminous face.
   Thine imperious eyes !
O the grief, O the grace,
   As of day when it dies.
Who is this bending over thee, lord, with tears and sup-
   pression of sighs ?

MELEAGER.

Is a bride so fair ?
Is a bride so meek ?
With unchapleted hair,
With unfilleted cheek,
Atalanta, the pure among women, whose name is as blessing
to speak.

ATALANTA.

I would that with feet
Unsandalled, unshod,
Overbold, overfleet,
I had swum not nor trod
From Arcadia to Calydon northward, a blast of the envy
of God.

The passages that follow are of no less memorable
beauty. The echoing sadness of the metre, the four
first lines tolling like a dirge, the fifth line sometimes
rising as a wail and escaping sometimes in the whisper
of a sigh ; the high enthusiasm, the almost Pythian
strangeness occasioned by the four antiphonal voices
answering each other across the gathering dusk ; the
impression of slow sacerdotal movement, the sense of
youth and death ; all these produce a cleansing of the
spirit, an almost overwhelming emotion of pity and
of fear.

The Kommos of *Atalanta* is in fact its conclusion.
There remains only the final exodos, the farewell
speech of Meleager. The nobility of this last lament
is marred by no faulty rhetoric ; the note of elevation
is maintained. There are those, indeed, who have
questioned the congruity of Meleager's final prayer
that Atalanta will close and kiss his eyelids when he is
gone. But if in fact this be a false intrusion of modern
sensibility, then surely it is redeemed by the high
restraint of Atalanta's own response, by the fine
aloofness of her ensuing departure :

> Hail thou : but I with heavy face and feet
> Turn homeward and am gone out of thine eyes.

And with that fall gently the six quiet chords of the epilogue.

In examining the amazing technique of *Atalanta in Calydon* it is well to make certain from the outset what was the main purpose which Swinburne had in mind. He himself, in his Dedicatory Epistle to the Collected Edition, defined this purpose as an " attempt to do something original in English which might in some degree reproduce for English readers the likeness of a Greek tragedy, with possibly something more of its true poetic life and charm than could have been expected from the authors of *Caractacus* and *Merope* ". Such a claim is modest enough, and should suffice at least to silence that school of criticism which condemns the style of *Atalanta* for its divergence in certain passages from the exact formulas and conception of a Greek drama. That such divergencies exist cannot, of course, be denied, and they were immediately selected and labelled by the critics of the time. Thus to Matthew Arnold the play appeared un-Greek in that it contained " too much beauty " ; Lowell referred to it as little more than a travesty of Hellenism ; and for Browning it was merely a " fuzz of words ". More serious, from the point of view of exact scholarship, was the criticism of such men as Thirlwall, who condemned as anachronistic the introduction of the romantic element as between Meleager and Atalanta, and who questioned those atheistic tirades which, even if permitted from the fevered lips of a Prometheus or a Cassandra, would never, at the best period of the Athenian stage, have been tolerated from the Chorus.

The fact is, however, and we may be grateful for it, that in this work at least Swinburne was attempting something more than a mere *pastiche* ; while retaining the ancient form and atmosphere, while exploiting the old tension between pity and terror, he had the wisdom and the courage to widen the scope of his drama by including the experiences of a later age. That he was justified in this decision is indubitable. The Greek dramatists could rely upon certain esoteric advantages which are denied to the modern author : their plays were produced in the honey-coloured theatre of Dionysus during the first hot days of spring, below the brow of the Acropolis, and to an audience already reverently disposed ; they were conducted according to a prescribed ritual, to flute and rhythmic dancing, with the unearthly immobility of masks and the rigid ungainliness of the cothurnus. These extraneous circumstances, the sun-warmed beauty of the setting, the receptive religious emotions of the audience, the detached unreality of the actors, did in fact contribute very materially to the " true poetic life and charm " of the old Greek plays. It is the skill with which Swinburne has been able artificially to recreate and maintain these three extraneous elements which renders *Atalanta* such a masterpiece of technique. Of the three, the sense of unreality was perhaps the easiest to evoke, since the very archaism of the form and language produces an impression not dissimilar from that of mask or buskin. The " religious " appeal is attained by the conflict between youth and death, joy and sorrow, hope and despair, free-will and predestination. But it is mainly in the creation of the wide external beauty of the Hellenic setting, in his substitutes for the effects of

lute and dancing, that Swinburne so splendidly out-
distances Matthew Arnold, and proves the comments
of that critic to have been so strangely beside the mark.

For the secret of *Atalanta* lies in the complete
response provoked in the poet by his own experience,
in the complete manner in which this experience is
conveyed. We have here no limited or specialised
experience : no merely fashionable aestheticism, no
trivial iridescence of green and silver. The beauty
herein experienced can be shared by any reader : it
produces not only a momentary thrill of emotion, but
a permanent modification of the structure of the mind ;
it represents an ordered adjustment, a symphonic
blending, of the impulses of light, of rhythm, and of
music. Light, in the very setting of the piece—the
first scenes of which, from the star-lit prologue of the
solitary huntsman to the final burst of morning in
Atalanta's opening words—

Sun and clear light among green hills—

are a vibrant crescendo of dawn. Light also in the
recurrent and interwoven theme of virginity, the flower-
bearing maidens of the Chorus, the silver-footed
Artemis, the swift white limbs of Atalanta. Light
also in the shining zest of Meleager, a virgin also,
about whom clings the freshness of his first adventure.
Rhythm in the meticulous balance and correlation of
each part, in the cadenced transitions from the major
to the minor key, in the continuous processional movement of the main choruses. And music, passionate,
unstrained, and haunting, in every line and lyric, as if
the whole action were accompanied by the throb of
hidden flutes—as if, in truth, the essential unity of the

drama were a lyric unity, a latent and continuous hymn to Dionysus.

By such perfection of technique Swinburne is able from the first to create full emotional sympathy between himself and the reader. This sympathy expands to something at once wider and deeper than mere emotion: the intelligence also is stimulated and satisfied ; a conviction is established that here at least Swinburne was able to realise, to co-ordinate, and to express the most intense, the most original, and the most various of his experiences. It is this completeness of mind which renders *Atalanta* the most valuable as well as the most communicable of all Swinburne's work. In his other poems, in " Hertha ", even, and in *Erechtheus*, we have an impression, not of direct and vividly apprehended experience, not of formative and co-ordinating imagination, but of a specialised and derivative belief. Whatever emotion such poems may provoke, they leave behind them a sense of incompleteness, a sense of some wastage of the poet's possibilities, a sense of frustration. In *Atalanta*, however, there are no such repressions : the experiences (sun, air, light, Greece, adolescence, virginity, courage, revolt, submission), the images which these provoke, are fused by the poet's imagination and discrimination into a single ordered whole ; the emotions of the reader being stirred and loosened culminate in an acute tension between the impulse of pity and the impulse of terror ; an almost intolerable problem of emotional adjustment is created; and with the solution of this problem through the co-ordinating force of the poet's imagination comes intense emotional relief, an attitude of liberation, an attitude, finally, of acquired balance.

For *Atalanta* is an event in the mind.

CHAPTER VI

WITH the publication of *Atalanta* Swinburne " shot like a rocket into celebrity ". The excitement was sectarian, but intense. They had all been expecting something ; and now it had happened—a white and blinding flash of lightning across that April sky. Never, it must be admitted, had the intelligentsia of England been so prepared, so anxious even, to be startled. For Tennyson, who had been an under-graduate heresy in 1832, and even in 1842, had since 1850 become merely a doctrine ; and in the *Enoch Arden* volume of 1864 he had shown the intellectuals that surprise at least was not one of the responses which the Laureate could be expected to provoke. And what they wanted, what they longed for, was to be surprised. Had not Mr. Ruskin been telling them to observe, to feel, and even to think for themselves ? What profit was there in being cultured, and sensitive, and broad-minded, if one's emotional adventures were to be merely of the tender variety, were to be understood by the vulgar, were to be appreciated even by the older generation ? The age was seeking for its heresies : it welcomed *Atalanta* with a tumult of acclaim. " The poetical atmosphere ", writes Professor Mackail, " was exhausted and heavy, like that of a sultry afternoon darkening to thunder. Out of the stagnation broke, as in a moment, the blaze and crash of *Atalanta in Calydon*. It was something quite new, quite unexampled. It revealed a new language in English, a new world, as it seemed, in Poetry."

There are signs also of a more intensive propaganda, of a more specific atmosphere for this success. The Pre-Raphaelites were at last becoming fashionable: what *The Germ* and even the *Defence of Guenevere* had failed to accomplish, had been achieved by Christina Rossetti's *Goblin Market* of 1862. By 1864 there were quite a number of people who began courageously to feel, and even to say, that the pictures of Millais, Burne-Jones, and Rossetti had "something to them", could not, that is, be dismissed as wholly ridiculous. Their conviction on this point was confirmed by the advocacy of Ruskin. The excitement of the new aestheticism began to spread in ever-widening circles. Several people had, even in 1862, noticed those curious poems by Algernon Swinburne in the *Spectator*. Lord Houghton, ubiquitous, kindly, authoritative, allowed no dinner-party (and there were many dinner-parties) to pass without a sympathetic reference to the new movement. Now Lord Houghton had been at Trinity with Tennyson: so he must be right. And here was Mr. Ruskin sending letters to people: "Have you read *Atalanta*? The grandest thing ever done by a youth—though he is a Demoniac youth." That in itself was exciting: and in this way the cream-coloured quarto of *Atalanta*, enriched by four gold medallions into which Rossetti had worked the symbol of the lotus flower, found its way to many a

London drawing-room, and was handled and discussed throughout that season of 1865.

All this was very bad for Swinburne. There is no doubt that from this moment, and for some years afterwards, he succumbed unduly to the excitement of success. He was lionised, and he liked being lionised; he would go to dinner - parties and get drunk and arrogant, and his voice would shrill up to a note of self-assertiveness which rendered him offensive to strangers, and which filled his friends with anguish, anxiety, and dismay. An unbound Prometheus, he would delight in adding astonishment to the surprise already occasioned; he would boast triumphantly of the variety and the deep-red colour of his vices—vices which he was pathetically incapable of practising, vices in which, if they had ever come to the point, he would have felt it unbecoming for an " English gentleman ", in spite of those French particles in his blood, actually to indulge. Yet throughout 1865 these habits grew upon Swinburne, and in December of that year they led to a highly unprepossessing incident. It was during one of Tennyson's periodic visits to London, and a meeting was arranged by Palgrave at which, before a select literary circle, the Laureate was for a second time to be confronted with the poet of the younger generation. It was unfortunate, perhaps, that this reunion was fixed for eleven in the evening, and that Swinburne had thus been allowed to dine alone. For on arrival he greeted Tennyson with his little stiff-backed Parisian bow, which in itself may well have clashed with the more rough-hewn Lincolnshire courtesies of the Laureate. The reverent circle had already formed in the main drawing-room around the

Laureate, and who knows whether, if things had gone more smoothly, there might not then have followed a short reading from *Maud* ? But things did not go smoothly. Ignoring the elder poet and the expectant circle which had formed around him, Swinburne strutted off to the back drawing-room, from where his voice, strident and self-assertive, could be heard raised in some wild monologue of his own. We may doubt whether, after this second meeting, the Laureate retained his previous impression of Swinburne as " a very modest and intelligent young fellow ". We know only that Houghton was seriously annoyed and administered a lecture which was much resented, and which three days later produced from Swinburne the following unrepentant and unconvincing letter :

22 DORSET STREET,
MY DEAR LORD HOUGHTON,   *Friday evening.*

As I do not doubt your kind intention, I will only ask Why ? When ? How ? Last time we met I had been spending the soberest of evenings here before starting to pick you up at 11 o'clock, which I understood was the order of the day. You as we returned seemed considerably infuriated with my unpunctuality—which I did not attribute to any influence of Bacchus on yourself. I am not aware of having retorted by any *discourtesy*. As the rest of the evening had been spent, after the few words of civility that passed between Mr. Tennyson and me, in discussing Blake and Flaxman in the next room with Palgrave and Lewes, I am at a loss to guess what has called down on me such an avalanche of advice. I have probably no vocation and doubtless no ambition for the service of Bacchus; in proof of which if you like I will undertake to repeat the conversation of Wednesday evening throughout with the accuracy of a reporter, as it happens to be fixed in my memory. . . . I remain, Yours affectionately,

A. C. SWINBURNE.

This dispute with Lord Houghton was doubly unfortunate : not only was he at that period the most reputable and helpful of all Swinburne's friends, but he was at that moment engaged in advising him in the selection of those poems which were then to be collected for publication under the title of *Poems and Ballads*. The coolness which arose between them after this unfortunate incident was soon dissipated, but a year or two later there occurred a further difference of opinion, and Swinburne lost thereby the advice and support of one who, by his intelligence and sympathy, had been enabled to exercise a wise and moderating influence.

Meanwhile he decided to publish *Chastelard*, the first play of what subsequently became his trilogy on Mary Queen of Scots. The early sketch of this play, written in the form of a dramatic poem, dates from his last year at Balliol. Since then it had been constantly on his mind : from time to time he would revert to it, altering or extending certain passages, according as his first uncritical enthusiasm for Mary Stuart was modified by more careful scrutiny and more scholarly research. So soon as the manuscript of *Atalanta* was off his hands he gave a final polish to *Chastelard*, and entrusted it to Moxon for publication.

Swinburne has confessed to an unreasoning romantic attachment to Mary Queen of Scots. In the " Adieux à Marie Stuart " which he published thirty years later he recalls his boyish enthusiasm in what is one of the best of his later poems :

> There beats no heart on either border
>   Wherethrough the north blasts blow
> But keeps your memory as a warder
>   His beacon-fire aglow.

H

> Long since it fired with love and wonder
>   Mine, for whose April age
> Blithe midsummer made banquet under
>   The shade of Hermitage.

This enthusiasm has its origin doubtless in the legend that one of his own ancestors, Sir Thomas Swinburne of Capheaton, had fallen in love with the Queen, and indeed taken up arms on her behalf. This early dynastic sympathy was fortified later by the study of the Pléiade, and by the discovery that Ronsard had himself, though at a respectful distance, been equally overcome. And, with the advent of manhood, Swinburne came to find in Mary Stuart the particular form of appeal which most attracted him :

> Éclair d'amour qui blesse et de haine qui tue,
> Fleur éclose au sommet du siècle éblouissant,
> Rose à tige épineuse et que rougit le sang.

His subsequent studies of her character obliged him, it is true, to modify this conception, and to admit that the main defect in Mary Stuart was not sensual cruelty but a feckless irresponsibility. At the moment, however, when he wrote, and even when he published, *Chastelard*, the earlier conception was still dominant, and the whole play therefore is based upon a theme which, although disguised by much beautiful writing, is none the less dominantly sensuous, and which contains in superabundance " soft things to feed sin's amorous mouth upon ". Obviously *Chastelard* is a disappointment after *Atalanta* : compared to that glittering white fountain of creation, it appears imitative, murky, almost dull. There is too much about it of the forced dramatic antithesis of *Hernani* and *Ruy Blas*. And yet it is a rapid, readable play. The first scene is admirable as a preparation : nor would it be easy, except in Shakespeare, to find a more skilful touch of indirect description than Mary Beaton's reference to her Queen :

> When she broke off the dance,
> Turning round short and soft—I never saw
> Such supple ways of walking as she has.

The culminating scene when Chastelard hides himself in Mary's marriage-chamber, a situation verging at every moment upon the ridiculous, is well managed and not wholly unconvincing ; while the last act, and particularly the description of Chastelard's execution, is certainly dramatic and, at moments, tragic. But the whole play is marred by its pervading tone of sensuality, an experience with which Swinburne was not himself familiar, or rather of which he was familiar only in a highly specialised and restricted sense. Thus Chastelard's monologue in prison, which might have excited the more durable emotions, is ruined by the dust and ashes of its conclusion :

> Ah, fair love,
> Fair fearful Venus made of deadly foam,
> I shall escape you somewhere with my death—
> Your splendid supple body and mouth on fire
> And Paphian breath that bites the lips with heat.
> I had best die.

A more serious breach of intellectual decorum is committed in the last act, at the moment when the Maids of Honour watching from a window at Holyrood have seen the axe descend. Mary Beaton, who is in love with Chastelard, has been crouching in the corner of the room. They call to her :

> MARY CARMICHAEL.
>
> Will you behold him dead ?

MARY BEATON.

Yea : must a dead man not be looked upon
That living one was fain of ?   Give me way.
Lo you, what sort of hair this fellow had ;
The doomsman gathers it into his hand
To grasp the head by for all men to see ;
I never did that.

MARY CARMICHAEL.

For God's love, let me go.

MARY BEATON.

I think sometimes she must have held it so,
Holding his head back, see you, by that hair
To kiss his face, still lying in his arms.

The passage is startling enough, and effective for
the moment.   But for the moment only, since surely
the intrusion of the physical at such a tragic crisis is
an error, not of taste merely, but of dramatic instinct.
For it was one of the more essential faults of Swinburne that he could never sacrifice a sensation of the
moment to the general scheme and unity of a complete
conception.

Apart from this basic defect, the play of *Chastelard*
is a fine piece of writing and construction.   The
character of Mary Queen of Scots, as then conceived
by Swinburne, is sketched with remarkable skill and
subtlety.   She is shown on the one hand as intensely
feminine, a soft " sea-witch ", frivolous, inconsequent,
a little frightened, intensely home-sick, almost pathetic ;
there hangs about her a certain imminence of tragedy,
a presentiment of her own sad death, the distant
murmur of the coming storm—" the base folk mutter-
ing like smoked bees ".   And on the other hand she is
hard, male, and ruthless :

> There's some blood in her
> That does not run to mercy as ours doth :
> That fair face and the cursed heart in her
> Made keener than a knife for manslaying
> Can bear strange things.

And predominantly hers also is the face that launched a thousand ships; to her also has been given the poisoned task to lure her lovers to destruction.   It is Chastelard himself who says :

> I know not : men must love even in life's spite ;
> For you will always kill them ; man by man
> Your lips will bite them dead : yea, though you would,
> You shall not spare one : all will die of you.

The manner, as distinct from the matter, of *Chastelard* provokes a more willing response.   The French lyrics are very skilful imitations of the Pléiade, marred only by Swinburne's incapacity for managing the vowel sounds of the French language, or for coping with the hiatus, a difficulty which presents itself to all foreign experimenters in that elusive medium.   The English lyrics, and especially Mary Beaton's song, " Between the sunset and the sea ", are of a far higher quality. The style of the dramatic portion reflects the influences of his undergraduate days ; there is much of the fore-shortening of Browning, there is much of the Rossetti sensuousness, and one phrase at least of direct Pre-Raphaelite suggestion :

> Seeing always in my sight I had your lips
> Curled over, red and sweet ; and the soft space
> Of carven brows, and splendour of great throat
> Swayed lily-wise.

But the technical interest of the style of *Chastelard* arises not so much from these reflections of past influences as from the clear evidence of what was about to come. For in many passages can be detected a recurrent note of *Poems and Ballads*.

Lord Houghton, that amiable and energetic man, had been endeavouring during the autumn of 1865 to ascertain whether or no the British public were in a fit state to welcome the publication of Swinburne's rapidly accumulating lyrics. After all, Palgrave and Ruskin had both heard the poems and had " accepted Swinburne's paganism with frankness ". Burne-Jones, Whistler, and Lady Trevelyan were also in favour of publication. Meredith, although he advised consider- able pruning, was not in principle opposed. Rossetti, who was becoming bored by the secret society of mutual admiration which was gathering round Algernon, was all for open diplomacy. Only Richard Burton hesitated ; for Burton knew (at least he thought he knew) exactly what most of the poems were about. One may question, indeed, whether any of the others, whether Ruskin in particular, shared this expert know- ledge : even Lord Houghton had, it seems, and without Swinburne's sanction, gaily offered the manuscript to John Murray, by whom of course it was indignantly rejected ; and when the tempest burst in August of 1866, Lord Houghton wrote quite mildly from Vichy, suggesting that all this panic and indignation were really very out of place.

The manuscript was entrusted to the firm of Edward Moxon & Co., at that time under the management of James Bertrand Payne. Payne, as Swinburne recorded subsequently, " was terribly nervous in those days ", which, when we consider that the firm had been heavily fined in 1841 for reissuing *Queen Mab*, is not wholly surprising. He decided in the first place on a *ballon d'essai* in the shape of a limited edition of " Laus Veneris " : the edition passed unperceived, and Moxons were reassured. The full collection was printed by the beginning of June, but the actual publication was delayed, owing to compositors' errors, till August. And it was then that the thunder crashed upon the frightened head of Bertrand Payne. Fearing prosecution, which was already being mooted in some quarters, he withdrew the volume from circulation, thus breaking his contract and enabling Swinburne, on the advice of his friends, to withdraw his copyrights from Moxon and to transfer them to the less reputable hands of John Camden Hotten. *Poems and Ballads* were thus again placed on the market in September. And the attacks continued.

In a famous passage of his *Life of Swinburne* Sir Edmund Gosse has described, by one of those expanding metaphors in the handling of which he is so inimitable, the reverberating sensation provoked by *Poems and Ballads*. " We see ", he writes, " the unquestioned genius of Tennyson in 1862 acting as a upas tree in English poetry, a widespread and highly popular growth beneath whose branches true imagination withers away. Propriety had prevailed ; and, once more to change our image, British poetry had become a beautiful guarded park in which, over smoothly shaven lawns, where gentle herds of fallow-deer were grazing, thrushes sang very discreetly from the boughs of ancestral trees, and where there was not a single object to be seen or heard which could offer the very smallest discomfort to the feelings of the most refined mid-Victorian gentlewoman. Into this quiet park, to the infinite alarm of the fallow-deer, a young

Bacchus was now preparing to burst, in the company of a troop of Maenads, and to the accompaniment of cymbals and clattering kettle-drums."

It would be to exceed the scope of this monograph were I to enter in any detail into the wild burst of disapprobation evoked by the publication of *Poems and Ballads*. Mr. John Morley's article in the *Saturday Review* of August 4, 1866, was the most intelligent, as well as one of the most violent, of the many protests. In this review Swinburne is spoken of as " an unclean fiery imp from the pit ", as " the libidinous laureate of a pack of satyrs ", and the pervading spirit of the poems is defined as being " the feverish carnality of a schoolboy over the dirtiest passages in Lemprière ".

There may be those to-day who, in re-reading *Poems and Ballads*, will agree with the late Lord Morley : our objections to the majority of the poems will, however, be based on intellectual and critical considerations rather than on any excessive prudery ; on regret, also, that the reputation of the author of *Atalanta* should have been cheapened by its association with the meretricious lechery of " Anactoria " or with the sadistic jingle of " Dolores " ; and as such, our strictures rest on a basis at once more durable and more important. We must remember, however, if we are to preserve our judgement against erroneous and disrespectful views of Swinburne, that *Poems and Ballads* were in their essence hymns of defiance, gestures of liberation, pæans of revolt. As subjective lyrical poems they are marred by the fault that will always render such poetry ephemeral : they are based on an experience which is neither permanent nor general. Pornography, as M. Lavedan has discovered, is not a

subject which the Muse can treat with any exhilaration ;
the supreme crises of physical sensation, followed as
they are by almost instantaneous reaction, are too
fugitive to provoke more than a superficial and temporary response. The experience in the most normal
circumstances is in itself exceptional, limited, blurred ;
its subsequent evocation can produce no fine emotional
vibration, no permanent appeal, and the poems which
deal with such matters become inevitably but " fugitive
things not good to treasure ". While this is true of
all poetry which deals exclusively with sensuality, the
seventeen studies of highly specialised sexual stimulations which figure among *Poems and Ballads* possess
the additional defect of being based on an experience
which is not only transitory but also eccentric. And
even then there is but little reticence or suggestion :
there is no fusion or interpretation. " From the
mysteries of religion ", wrote Landor, " the veil is
seldom to be drawn, from the mysteries of love never.
For this offence the gods take away from us our freshness of heart and our susceptibilities of pure delight."
It is regrettable that Swinburne, who absorbed so
much from Landor, should have failed to absorb this
doctrine also.

His own defence, the defence which he published
in *Poems and Reviews*, is sufficiently disingenuous to be
really amusing. The contention that they are merely
experiments in dramatic monologues—that " Dolores ",
which, in writing to his friend Howell, he had himself
referred to as " the perennial and poisonous fountain
of Dolores ", is merely the first of a sedate trilogy, and
" Anactoria " but an adaptation of Sappho and one
which contains no single indecent passage—evokes a

welcome smile. It is only at the end of his apologia that Swinburne indicates what is the only possible justification for these poems, namely, that they represent a protest against the idyllic and tender optimism of Tennyson. On such grounds it is possible, indeed, to base a defence, which gives them not merely an intellectual reason for existence, but an actual coherence and meaning. If taken merely as crackers fired impishly to startle his contemporaries out of the domestic idyll, then they are acceptable enough : one would wish only that they had been conceived with more indignation and less obvious enjoyment, or at least in metres of less seductive brilliance, by which their meritorious objective purpose has been obscured. For such a purpose did in truth exist. The windmills at which Swinburne tilted with such reckless exuberance have, it must be realised, long since disappeared. But they existed in 1865. Although to us the flame which blazed into *Poems and Ballads* may seem but as the crackling of dried bracken, yet at the time there were many tangled thickets, such as *The Angel in the House*, which it was useful for Swinburne thus to extirpate. We see to-day only the dead vestiges of ash around his bonfire ; we do not see the choking growth of brambles through which he blazed a trail. For us the blood-stained sensuality of *Poems and Ballads* appears to have served but little purpose—to have led at its best to Flecker, and at its worst to Wilde. But we must never forget that to many sensible people in 1866 these hectic poems echoed as a bugle in the night-time, that they blazed for lost wayfarers as a beacon lighted on some higher hill. And with fitting humility we must recognise that our very misunderstanding of the situation—our actual inability to visualise the thick undergrowths which once encumbered our fair fields of ease and liberty—are due to the completeness, the explosive rapidity, with which Swinburne accomplished his task.   For the value of dynamite should be tested by the weight of accumulated matter which it is able, suddenly, to remove.

The arrangement and order of the poems incorporated in this the first published volume of Swinburne's lyrical verse is curiously unsystematic.   He himself contended that some of the poems dated from his Eton period : this is certainly untrue.   We may take it, however, that such obviously early experiments as " Aholibah " and " Madonna Mia " date from 1858. The two political poems, " A Song in Time of Order " and " A Song in Time of Revolution ", must also have been composed during his last year at Balliol.   Between April and September 1862 seven of the pieces which figure in *Poems and Ballads* appeared in the *Spectator*, notably " Faustine ", " The Sundew ", " August ", "After Death", and "Before Parting".   We know also that the " Laus Veneris ", the " Triumph of Time ", the "Ballad of Life", and the "Ballad of Death", and probably " Les Noyades " and " A Leave-taking ", belong to the same year.   We may assume that those poems and ballads in which the Pre-Raphaelite influence is predominant, such as " Dorothy ", " The Two Dreams", " The King's Daughter", " In the Orchard", "April ", "A Christmas Carol ", and " The Masque of Queen Bersabe ", were composed before the year 1863. From the spring of 1863 dates the "Hermaphroditus", from 1864 " Itylus " and " Félise ", and from 1865 " Dolores " and the " Ode to Victor Hugo ".   The remaining dates, to say the least, are uncertain.

It will be best, therefore, to divide the poems not according to the assumed dates of their composition, but into the main categories suggested by their form or subject matter. A rough classification might be made as follows :

I. *Pre-Raphaelite.*

Ballad of Life.
Ballad of Death.
Madonna Mia.
In the Orchard.
April.
August.
A Christmas Carol.
Ballad of Burdens.
After Death.
May Janet.
The Bloody Son.
The Sea-swallows.

II. *Incidental and Decorative, but mainly under the Pre-Raphaelite influence.*

Aholibah.
Masque of Queen Bersabe.
Itylus.
Song before Death.
Stage Love.
Before the Mirror.
Love at Sea.
The Sundew.
An Interlude.
A Match. (The last stanza of which might place it in section VIII.)

III. *Dramatic Monologues.*

Félise.
The Leper.
At Eleusis.

IV. *Political.*

> Song in Time of Order.
> Song in Time of Revolution.

V. *Complimentary Odes.*

> Ode to Victor Hugo.
> Ode to Landor.

VI. *Classical and Experimental.*

> Phaedra.
> Hendecasyllabics.

VII. *Poems on Death and Mortality.*

> Hymn to Proserpine.
> Ilicet.
> A Litany.
> A Lamentation.
> Anima Anceps.

VIII. *Poems of Passion.*

> Laus Veneris.
> Hermaphroditus.
> Faustine.
> Dolores : Garden of Proserpine : Hesperia.
> Anactoria.
> Fragoletta.
> Satia te Sanguine.
> A Cameo.
> Rococo.
> Erotion.
> Before Dawn.
> Before Parting.
> Sapphics.
> Love and Sleep.
> The Year of Love.
> Les Noyades.

IX. *Poems of Direct Experience.*

> The Triumph of Time.
> A Leave-taking.

The above classification, arbitrary though it be, is of value if only because it limits the subsequent field of discussion, and allows the poems to fall into a certain perspective. The verses of the first category are little more than brilliant imitations of the work of others : how brilliant and how exact is this imitation may be gauged by the following crystallisation of the Pre-Raphaelite manner :

> She held a little cithern by the strings,
>> Shaped heartwise, strung with subtle-coloured hair
>> Of some dead lute-player
> That in dead years had done delicious things.
> The seven strings were named accordingly :
>> The first string charity,
>>> The second tenderness,
> The rest were pleasure, sorrow, sleep and sin,
> And loving-kindness, that is pity's kin
>> And is most pitiless.

The second category need scarcely detain us. " Aholibah " is a rather feckless expansion of Ezekiel ; " The Masque of Queen Bersabe " contains the famous parade of queens, each one attired in the manner of Gustave Moreau ; " The Sundew " and the " Interlude " have an unexpectedly idyllic flavour. The third category, that of the dramatic monologues, is also derivative, although it must be admitted that the tone of " Félise " is extremely personal. The general conception, however, proceeds from such poems of Browning as " A Lover's Quarrel " and " The Worst of It ". " At Eleusis " recalls Browning's " Artemis prologises ", while " The Leper " is almost as macabre as Tennyson's " Happy ", which it may possibly have suggested. The two political odes are, in comparison to *Songs before Sunrise*, immature in quality, while the classical experiments are of no outstanding interest, the

" Hendecasyllabics ", all in the dainty metre of Catullus,
being, however, exceedingly accomplished. Of the two
complimentary odes, that to Landor must have a place
to itself among the many similar poems which Swinburne subsequently composed. For here the experience
is wider and more human than in his other literary
eulogies, having about it something of the short sharp
freshness of an early Florentine spring. The seventh
category, those poems which in a mood of satiety and
despair sing of death either as the final cruelty or the
final release, are of a far less transitory quality. " A
Litany " and " Lamentation " are odes on the cruelty
of Fate and God which echo the note of despairing
resignation which we have already noticed in the
choruses of Atalanta. " Ilicet " is a lament on the
passage of time and the purposelessness of human
existence, reflecting in gentler measures the sudden
indignant outbursts of FitzGerald's *Omar* :

> In deep wet ways by grey old gardens,
> Fed with sharp spring the sweet fruit hardens ;
>   They know not what fruits wane or grow ;
> Red summer burns to the utmost ember ;
> They know not, neither can remember,
>   The old years and flowers they used to know.

The haunting, satiated melody of the " Hymn to
Proserpine ", its audacious paganism, have given it a
prominence which it does not intrinsically merit : as
an exercise in metrics, as a study even in shimmering
atmosphere, it is a masterpiece ; as a philosophical
poem it is merely meretricious. Far more memorable
is the lovely lament of " Anima Anceps ", although as
so often with Swinburne the images are not co-
ordinated, and the metre exercises a marked hypnotic
effect :

If one day's sorrow
Mar the day's morrow—
If man's life borrow
    And man's death pay—
If souls once taken,
If lives once shaken,
Arise, awaken,
    By night, by day—
Why with strong crying
And years of sighing,
Living and dying,
    Fast ye and pray ?
For all your weeping,
Waking and sleeping,
Day comes to reaping
    And takes away.

The eighth category has been labelled " Poems of Passion " ; and an explanation has been given why it is so regrettable that these particular verses should have spread their tone and colour not only over the collection in which they appear, but even, for the unwary, over the whole mass of Swinburne's lyrical work. Except from the purely prosodic point of view, there are none of them of durable interest.   Their beauty, intoxicating though it be, is one to which the emotions only can react ; they represent but an ephemeral, even momentary stage in Swinburne's own development. Their inspiration arises, as W. M. Rossetti has recorded, from " one of the less genuine constituents of the author's mind " ; or, as Swinburne himself explained with admirable and convincing simplicity, " the impulse ceased ".

It may be noted, perhaps, as curiously significant that the best of these poems of passion are inspired either by art or literature.   Swinburne's direct sexual experience was, to say the least, no very potent or pregnant impulse ; it is only when he is able to receive this impulse through the conductor of other, and to him more intrinsic, experiences that it provokes anything more than a purely superficial response. Thus the " Hermaphroditus ", suggested by the statue in the Louvre as well as by a passage in Shelley's " Witch of Atlas ", is obviously a less fugitive performance than " Dolores " ; whereas " Fragoletta ", inspired partly by a Giorgione drawing and perhaps, also, as M. Reul has discovered, by the novel of Hector de Latouche, has a low wistful note which places it on a level far above the companion pieces of strident sexuality :

> O bitterness of things too sweet !
> O broken sighing of the dove !
> Love's wings are over-fleet,
> And like the panther's feet
> The feet of Love.

" Faustine ", also, that " chanson cruelle et câline ", for all its blood and sand, has a certain enduring quality which may well be due to the fact that its origin was partly derivative, that it was suggested by the profile of the Roman Empress upon a coin. And even " Anactoria ", a maenad poem doubtless, contains one passage at least by which the interest is seriously aroused, but it is a passage in which Sappho, his school-boy heroine, is addressing her own literary reputation and not ranting about the physical charms of Gyrinna, Atthis, and the rest :

> Men shall not see bright fire nor hear the sea,
> Nor mix their hearts with music, nor behold
> Cast forth of heaven, with feet of awful gold
> And plumeless wings that make the bright air blind,
> Lightning, with thunder for a hound behind
> Hunting through fields unfurrowed and unsown,
> But in the light and laughter, in the moan

I

> And music, and in grasp of lip and hand
> And shudder of water that makes felt on land
> The immeasurable tremor of all the sea,
> Memories shall mix and metaphors of me.
> Like me shall be the shuddering calm of night,
> When all the winds of the world for pure delight
> Close lips that quiver and fold up wings that ache ;
> When nightingales are louder for love's sake,
> And leaves tremble like lute-strings or like fire ;
> Like me the one star swooning with desire
> Even at the cold lips of the sleepless moon,
> As I at thine ; like me the waste white noon,
> Burnt through with barren sunlight ; and like me
> The land-stream and the tide-stream in the sea.

Passages such as these, the sudden strong-winged escape from " the senses and the sorrows and the sins ", recur throughout the poems, giving to them the salt, sad savour of a tideless sea. For even as to Tannhäuser in Mount Horsel there is no gaiety in all this viciousness :

> Harsh springs and fountains bitterer than the sea,
> Grief a fixed star, and joy a vane that veers.

A brooding satiety aches in every line, lending even to " Dolores " what M. Reul has finely called " la nostalgie d'un idéal ", giving a sense of utter weariness :

I am sick of singing ; the bays burn deep and chafe : I am fain
To rest a little from praise and grievous pleasure and pain ;

a dumb longing for escape, by death if need be :

> From too much love of living,
>   From hope and fear set free,
> We thank with brief thanksgiving
>   Whatever gods may be
> That no life lives for ever ;
> That dead men rise up never ;
> That even the weariest river
>   Winds somewhere safe to sea.

a constant yearning for light, for sunshine, for the sea :

> Ah yet would God this flesh of mine might be
> Where air might wash and long leaves cover me,
>   Where tides of grass break into foam of flowers,
> Or where the wind's feet shine along the sea.

I have kept to the last the two poems of this volume which shine out from the rest with the clear light of direct and deeply realised experience. It will be remembered that " The Triumph of Time " was written in 1862 at the moment when Swinburne was smarting from the cruel climax of his one romance. " He assured me ", writes Sir Edmund Gosse, " that the stanzas of this wonderful lyric represented with the exactest fidelity the emotions which passed through his mind when his anger had died down and when nothing remained but the infinite pity and the pain." " A Leave-taking " and I fear also " Les Noyades " are similarly inspired by this incident. But at least " The Triumph of Time " and " A Leave-taking " are two of the finest lyrics in the language, and worth in themselves the whole orchestra of *Poems and Ballads*. There are fourteen stanzas in the former poem which are redundant, and which mar the symmetry of the whole : the technical perfection of the latter poem is, however, complete :

> Let us go hence, my songs ; she will not hear.
> Let us go hence together without fear ;
> Keep silence now, for singing-time is over,
> And over all old things and all things dear.
> She loves not you nor me as all we love her.
> Yea, though we sang as angels in her ear,
>   She would not hear.

Through both poems there runs a note of wounded dignity, of sorrowful forgiveness, of stoical reserve, which provokes a more sympathetic response than any

of the plangent ecstatics of his other laments.   For he
is bewailing not the loss of happiness only but the
withered hope of redemption :

> I have given no man of my fruit to eat ;
>   I trod the grapes, I have drunken the wine.
> Had you eaten and drunken and found it sweet,
>   This wild new growth of the corn and vine,
> This wine and bread without lees or leaven,
> We had grown as gods, as the gods in heaven,
> Souls fair to look upon, goodly to greet,
>   One splendid spirit, your soul and mine.

For here at least had appeared the sure escape from
" sick dreams and sad of a dull delight ", the hope of a
new freshness and a purer strength.   And now only a
relapse is possible, a further plunge to hide himself still
deeper in that final Malebolge where even pity will not
seek him out.

There is no vituperation in his despair : no feeble
snivelling : it is with pathetic generosity, a very noble
courage, that he writes :

> You have chosen and clung to the chance they sent you,
>   Life sweet as perfume and pure as prayer,
> But will it not one day in heaven repent you ?
>   Will they solace you wholly, the days that were ?
> Will you lift up your eyes between sadness and bliss,
> Meet mine, and see where the great love is,
> And tremble and turn and be changed ?   Content you ;
>   The gate is strait : I shall not be there.

The technical skill of this stanza, the way that the
anapaests are snapped suddenly by the little mono-
syllables of the last line, is a fit preparation for the
magnificent finale, the full diapason of which is, however, interrupted in the original by the insertion of
twelve otiose and redundant stanzas :

I will go back to the great sweet mother,
    Mother and lover of men, the sea.
I will go down to her, I and none other,
    Close with her, kiss her and mix her with me :
Cling to her, strive with her, hold her fast :
O fair white mother, in days long past
Born without sister, born without brother,
    Set free my soul as thy soul is free.

I shall sleep, and move with the moving ships,
    Change as the winds change, veer in the tide ;
My lips will feast on the foam of thy lips,
    I shall rise with thy rising, with thee subside ;
Sleep, and not know if she be, if she were,
Filled full with life to the eyes and hair,
As a rose is fulfilled to the roseleaf tips
    With splendid summer and perfume and pride.

     .   .   .   .   .   .

I shall go my ways, tread out my measure,
    Fill the days of my daily breath
With fugitive things not good to treasure,
    Do as the world doth, say as it saith ;
But if we had loved each other—O sweet,
Had you felt, lying under the palms of your feet,
The heart of my heart, beating harder with pleasure
    To feel you tread it to dust and death—

Ah, had I not taken my life up and given
    All that life gives and the years let go,
The wine and honey, the balm and leaven,
    The dreams reared high and the hopes brought low ?
Come life, come death, not a word be said ;
Should I lose you living, and vex you dead ?
I never shall tell you on earth ; and in heaven,
    If I cry to you then, will you hear or know ?

CHAPTER VII

" SONGS BEFORE SUNRISE ", 1871

THE scandal aroused by *Poems and Ballads* reverberated throughout England and beyond. The world of letters was shaken as though by an earthquake. Even in America, where the book had been published by Messrs. Carleton in the early autumn of 1866, the controversy blazed into a nine days' wonder. The name of Swinburne became a word subversive in many households. His success was such that the editor of *Punch* for once lost his temper and wrote a vicious paragraph on Mr. " Swineborn "; that Mr. G. F. Watts asked him to sit for the picture which is now in the National Portrait Gallery, and refused to permit him to cut his hair, " whose curls ", Swinburne wrote, " the British public (unlike Titian's) reviles aloud in the streets ". Mr. John Camden Hotten was not slow to take professional advantage of this blaze of notoriety ; he induced Swinburne to publish not only the Notes on *Poems and Reviews* which I have already mentioned, but a purely fugitive poem on a drawing by F. Sandys entitled " Cleopatra " which Meredith had condemned as a " farrago of the most obvious commonplaces " of Swinburne's ordinary style. Mr. Hotten did not, however, succeed in obtaining the two poetical satires, and notably the longer satire on J. A. Froude, which were written in connection with *Poems and Reviews* and which figure only in Mr. Wise's bibliography.

The success of *Poems and Ballads* was not, it must be noted, solely a *succès de scandale*. There were many serious critics who, being hypnotised by the immense technical and communicative merits which the poems then possessed, saw in them an actual value permanent and creative ; they wrote as if they were welcoming the dawn of a new era in English poetry. It is important for us, who regard Swinburne as coming at the end of a long poetic tradition, to realise that to his contemporaries he appeared to be the pioneer of a new movement. It is this which explains how in 1869 the *Temps* could refer to Swinburne as the greatest living English poet ; how Victor Hugo could press Paul Meurice to translate the poems for the *Rappel* ; and how, strangest of all, Ruskin could refuse to join Mr. Ludlow's movement for a criminal prosecution in terms so definite and so unexpected as the following :

He is infinitely above me in all knowledge and power, and I should no more think of advising him or criticising him than of venturing to do it to Turner if he were alive again. . . . He is simply one of the mightiest scholars of the age in Europe . . . in power of imagination and understanding he simply sweeps me away before him as a torrent over a pebble. I'm *righter* than he is—so are the lambs and the swallows, but they're not his match.

We have seen how the plaudits which greeted *Atalanta* had induced a mood of arrogance and intractability ; the shouts and hisses which arose upon the appearance of *Poems and Ballads* led to a prolonged

attack of anti-social behaviour. Swinburne's relations
with his older and more reputable friends became
intermittent and self-conscious. Lady Trevelyan had
died in the spring of 1866 ; Richard Burton had
accepted a consular appointment in South America ;
the intimacy with Rossetti, with Burne-Jones even,
had somewhat cooled ; Swinburne quarrelled with
Whistler ; his attitude towards Lord Houghton became
one of defiant irritability, culminating during the years
that followed in a definite but not lasting estrangement ;
only with his new-found cronies was he really at his
ease, only with Charles Howell and Solomon did he
cease to be on the defensive. To the former he sub-
mitted the management of his mundane affairs ; this
was an unwise proceeding, for Howell, that strangely
vicious Anglo-Portuguese, was not in any sense of
the term reliable. Even less reputable, though no less
picturesque, was Simeon Solomon, the Marcellus of
the Pre-Raphaelite movement, but already in 1867
clouded by that fog of alcohol and degradation through
which, after a period as a pavement artist in Bayswater,
he shambled to the workhouse. A more respectable,
though scarcely less deleterious, friend of these years
was George Powell, with whom Swinburne now became
on the terms of the closest intimacy. It is not necessary
to examine in any detail the depressing interlude which
stretches in Swinburne's biography from the publication
of *Poems and Ballads* in 1866 to the appearance of *Songs
before Sunrise* in 1871. The satiety which is implicit
in so many poems of the earlier volume produced no
immediately permanent reaction : it was not till 1879
at the age of forty-two that Swinburne broke definitely
with his own past ; nor need the repudiation of the

Prelude to *Songs before Sunrise* be accorded any very literal interpretation.

Of outward events there is little to record.   In 1867 he was placed in connection with the American school-teacher and actress Adah Isaacs Menken, a stalwart, serviceable lady, who had already been married five times, on one occasion to the pugilist John Heenan, and who was then, with astounding acrobatic efficiency, performing at Astley's Circus in the then popular spectacle entitled *Mazeppa*.   Strapped to a circus-horse, her hair curled and shingled in the Byronic manner, she would lollop round the ring waving with graceful agility a sword and buckler.   It is questionable whether, in spite of Rossetti's friendly encouragement, the poet in any very active manner responded to the advances of this Artemis.   " Good old Menken ", he called her in his letters of the period.   " She was ", he wrote later, " lovable as a friend as well as a mistress." Such praise rings unconvincing in comparison to Mrs. Menken's own " Infelicia ", which she dedicated to Charles Dickens and induced Mr. Hotten to publish in 1868 ; but it accords well enough with the ribald caricatures with which Burne-Jones celebrated the episode and which are now in the possession of Mr. Wise.   And in the summer of 1868 Mrs. Menken proceeded to Paris, where she died.

Throughout these years Swinburne was subject to the recurrence of those strange fits which so disturbed all beholders : on one occasion he collapsed at Lord Houghton's breakfast table, on another he was seen by the young Edmund Gosse being carried in a chair through the corridors of the British Museum, " a *cupido crucifixus* on a chair of anguish ".   His family, who by then had left the Isle of Wight for Holmwood near Henley on Thames, became seriously alarmed. Again and again the Admiral would be telegraphed for and would arrive in time to rescue his son from what seemed a final collapse. At Holmwood he would quickly recuperate, and even in London the friendly advice and assistance of Burton's friend, Dr. Bird, often protected him from the worst results of his excesses. In the summer he would go to Étretat, where George Powell had rented a cottage. It may be doubted perhaps whether this *villégiature* was as salutary as the Admiral and Dr. Bird imagined : the little house was christened by Swinburne " la chaumière de Dolmancé ", as a tribute to the *Justine* of M. de Sade ; but we may question whether Dr. Bird, in spite of his intimacy with Burton, was able to identify the allusion. It was there that the young and imaginative De Maupassant visited him in the summer of 1868, and it was at Étretat also that in the same summer he was nearly drowned. The story of this wellnigh fatal adventure is vividly recorded by Sir Edmund Gosse in his *Portraits and Sketches*.

It is not to be imagined, however, that during this period Swinburne had become intellectually as well as physically torpid. It is true indeed that between the years 1866 and 1871 he published no poetical collection of outstanding importance. " A Song of Italy " dates from 1867, and the " Appeal to England " was issued in the same year. " Siena " and " Notes on the Royal Academy " were published in 1868, and in August of that year appeared the impressive and admirable critical volume on *Blake*. The " Ode on the Proclamation of the French Republic " was issued by F. S. Ellis in

September 1870, Swinburne having by then quarrelled with J. C. Hotten.   Moreover, had it not been for this quarrel, *Songs before Sunrise* might well have appeared in 1870 : it was merely because Hotten threatened legal proceedings that publication was so long delayed.   A large number of the poems had by then already appeared in the *Fortnightly Review*, under the editorship of John Morley.   In December 1866 Swinburne was introduced to Morley by Joseph Knight, and from January of the next year until as late as 1892 he became a regular contributor to the *Fortnightly*.   These contributions, whether they took the form of original poems or of essays in criticism, are important in that they maintained public interest in the poet during a period in which, to judge only by his published books, he would seem to have remained comparatively dumb.   Thus among other poems the fine memorial ode to Baudelaire first appeared in the *Fortnightly* for January 1868, and a whole series of critical monographs followed.   Nor were these his only activities.   He finished, but never published, a novel entitled *Lesbia Brandon*, and throughout this period he was working on *Bothwell*, the first act of which was completed by 1868.

In spite, however, of these proofs of industry his friends were distressed and anxious.   There was something so childlike and unnecessary about Swinburne's vices and ventures that his more sincere admirers felt it their duty to rescue him from the Howells and the Solomons of life, and at least to set before him " a conscience and an aim ".   Sir Edmund Gosse has recorded that, as early as March 1867, a meeting was convoked by Jowett to discuss " what could be done *with* and *for* Algernon ".   This council was held at the

house of George Howard ; Mazzini himself was present.
They showed him the " Ode to Candia " ; undeterred
by that windy production, Mazzini agreed to come to
the rescue ; he promised to write to the young poet
and to enlist his services in the case of the People's
Republic. From the first, the unfailing psychological
instinct of Jowett was justified : Swinburne flamed
instantaneously to the match thus applied. It was
Karl Blind who finally arranged an interview between
Swinburne and Mazzini. " I did ", the former
recorded later, " as I always thought I should and really
meant not to do if I could help—went down on my
knees and kissed his hand." One's sympathy, on
this occasion, goes out to Mazzini : embarrassed and
bewildered he had to sit there and listen to the
" Song of Italy " ; to hear the shrill ecstatic voice
rising octave by octave under the stress of that
torrential doxology ; names here and there emerging
suddenly like palings in a flood — Brescia, Majano,
Fonte Branda ; his own name about him suddenly
in the hurricane :

> Mazzini,—O our prophet, O our priest,
> A little while at least. . . .

Certainly a trying ordeal ; but one, after all, which led
directly to *Songs before Sunrise*.

In " Thalassius " and the Prelude to *Songs before
Sunrise* Swinburne represented himself as having
renounced for ever the violent delights of his youth for
the austere serenities of Liberty and Nationalism ;
this renunciation, as we have seen, was optative rather
than actual. It is not to be supposed, however, that
these hopes and these intentions were anything but

sincere. " Other books ", he would say, " are books :
Songs before Sunrise is myself."   And indeed there can
be no question but that his hero-worship, his passion
for Landor, Victor Hugo, and Mazzini, represented a
very deep-seated impulse towards the ideal : that to
him the love of Liberty, the hatred of all despotism,
fusing with these gods of his idolatry, constituted an
ever-present religion ; and that in some confused but
persistent manner these sun-lit aspirations and enthusiasms, this delicious tension between struggle and
submission, were symbolised for him by the sea,
illimitable and forgiving, the source for him of all
brighter energies, the constant metaphor for health and
freedom, the final ablution of all sullen sins.   This
aspect of his regeneration is implicit in the whole theme
of " Thalassius ", and is summarised in three beautiful
stanzas of the " Prelude " :

> Between the bud and the blown flower
> Youth talked with joy and grief an hour,
>   With footless joy and wingless grief
>   And twin-born faith and disbelief
> Who share the seasons to devour ;
>   And long ere these made up their sheaf
> Felt the winds round him shake and shower
>   The rose-red and the blood-red leaf,
> Delight whose germ grew never grain,
> And passion dyed in its own pain.
>
> Then he stood up, and trod to dust
> Fear and desire, mistrust and trust,
>   And dreams of bitter sleep and sweet,
>   And bound for sandals on his feet
> Knowledge and patience of what must
>   And what things may be, in the heat
> And cold of years that rot and rust
>   And alter ; and his spirit's meat
> Was freedom, and his staff was wrought
> Of strength, and his cloak woven of thought.

For what has he whose will sees clear
To do with doubt and faith and fear,
　　Swift hopes and slow despondencies ?
　　His heart is equal with the sea's
And with the sea-wind's, and his ear
　　Is level to the speech of these,
And his soul communes and takes cheer
　　With the actual earth's equalities,
Air, light and night, hills, winds and streams,
And seeks not strength from strengthless dreams.

It is clear, indeed, from this important poem that Swinburne was himself aware of how fugitive and at the same time how limited was the central theme of *Poems and Ballads* : that he himself had realised that no work of art can be based solely on an appeal to animalism, and that the flame of poetry must of necessity be kindled from wider and less eccentric experiences.

It is in this sense that *Songs before Sunrise* represent an endeavour to respond to some more durable and less individual stimulus. To their making came absolute sincerity, passionate conviction, enthusiastic idealism, the sunlight of love, and the burning heat of hatred : all this invested with the glowing colours of unequalled imagery, and set to the vibration of unimaginable music. And yet, for all their radiance, *Songs before Sunrise* do not always rise to the level of their opportunity ; it is only at rare moments that the reader is convincingly stirred by all these rhapsodies ; it is only at rare intervals that his interest, or even his attention, can respond. There is almost throughout an obstruction of communication, a sense of wastage. In *Atalanta* Swinburne had drawn to the full on his experience, had released all his repressions, and had yet kept control. In the majority of *Songs before*

Sunrise he draws only on a specialised experience, releases but few repressions, and loses control after the first two stanzas. The reader does not even feel the necessity of emotional adjustment ; for his emotions are not engaged.

The thirty-eight poems collected in this volume may be divided into two main divisions, namely, " Songs of Revolution " and " Hymns to Liberty ". The first division is primarily topical and deals with the condition of Europe between 1867 and 1871. The second division is primarily philosophical and represents an endeavour to define the relations between the abstract conception of Liberty and the soul of man. A more detailed classification may be given as follows :

I. SONGS OF THE RISORGIMENTO.

1. *Topical.*

> The Halt before Rome.
> Mentana : First anniversary.
> Blessed among Women.   (Signora Cairoli.)
> Insurrection in Candia.

2. *Elegiacs for Italy.*

> Super Flumina Babylonis.
> Siena.
> Song of the Standard.
> Non dolet.

3. *Appeals for World-revolution.*

> The Eve of Revolution.
> A Watch in the Night.
> Litany of Nations.
> Quia Multum Amavit.
> A Marching Song.

4. *Invectives against England.*

> To Walt Whitman in America.
> An Appeal.
> Perinde ac Cadaver.

5. *Invectives against the Church.*

> Before a Crucifix.
> Christmas Antiphones.

6. *The Workers.*

> Tenebrae.   (Hope.)
> The Pilgrims.   (Sacrifice.)
> The Oblation.   (Sacrifice.)
> Messidor.   (Co-operation.)
> Monotones.   (Patience.)

7. *The Leaders.*

> Armand Barbès.
> Eurydice.   (V. Hugo.)
> Cor Cordium.   (Shelley.)
> A New Year's Message.   (Mazzini.)
> Epilogue.   (Mazzini.)

II. HYMNS TO LIBERTY

1. *Liberty as the Mother of Man.*

> Mater Dolorosa.
> Mater Triumphalis.

2. *Liberty as the New Dawn.*

> On the Downs.
> Tiresias.

3. *Liberty as Faith.*

> A Year's Burden.

4. *Liberty as the Soul of Man.*
> Genesis.
> Hymn of Man.
> Hertha.

Now whereas all the poems in the second of these two categories are fine and memorable, the greater proportion of those comprised in the first category are wearisome and unconvincing ; for the Songs of the *Risorgimento* are for obvious reasons based on an experience which is transitory, vicarious, almost parasitic, whereas the Hymns to Liberty make a more permanent and more universal appeal and penetrate deeper into Swinburne's own nervous system. This distinction is of great importance if we are to obtain from the *Songs before Sunrise* any useful response, and it will be of advantage perhaps to emphasise the distinction by an examination of the technical merits and defects of the collection as a whole.

Sir Edmund Gosse, while being a convinced admirer of the poems, admits that the " apparent causelessness of the emotion, and the vain violence as of a whirlwind in a vacuum, add to our difficulty in placing ourselves in a sensitive relation with a noble body of poetry ". This difficulty, and it is a real one, will to some extent be mitigated if the distinction above indicated is borne in mind, and if the poems of the second category are read with vigilance, and those of the first category enjoyed merely for their metrical and other adventitious qualities. For it is in the first category that the " causelessness of the emotion " exercises so narcotic an influence. There is in the first place the exhausting exaggeration of enthusiasm : except in one or two poems, such as " Before a Crucifix " and " On the

K

Downs ", in both of which there is a welcome gradation, Swinburne begins at once on the top note ; he allows himself no scope for crescendo, he allows the reader no occasion for the exercise of his own interpretative faculties. This unfortunate insistence is rendered even more unpalatable by the biblical language so predominantly employed, by the almost revivalist attitude adopted by the poet, by the shrill rhetoric in which he claims the functions of a prophet. Hugo, it is true, could say with conviction, " Je fais mon métier de flambeau ", but the reader is not fully convinced when Swinburne claims a similar vocation :

> I am the trumpet at thy lips, thy clarion
>   Full of thy cry, sonorous with thy breath ;
> The graves of souls born worms and creeds grown carrion
>   Thy blast of judgment fills with fires of death.

We might, indeed, accept all this exaggeration were we convinced that Swinburne's excitement was anything more than purely cerebral. But we are not so convinced. He had been only twice to Italy for a few weeks ; he had no interests there ; he was in no way personally identified with the *Risorgimento* ; his emotion was thus purely vicarious, it was " infiltrated and permeated by Mazzini ". But even here, the stimulus does not wholly justify the resultant convulsions. For in principle hero-worship carried to such excess is no very normal emotion, nor is it based upon any permanent or general human experience. It is eccentric, or at best sectarian ; it makes no wide appeal to the healthy intelligence. And finally, these political poems are not even accurate as a rendering of the then existent problems of the Italian situation : Swinburne writes of the events of 1867 in the spirit of 1848 ; the unreality of the experience is thereby intensified.

It is not surprising, therefore, that the reader of to-day should be disconcerted by such abnormal excitement as inspires the impassioned personification of Italy in the twenty-second stanza of " The Eve of Revolution ", or that the poem addressed to Signora Cairoli should seem to stand in no relation to the apparent circumstances of Swinburne's experience. This impression can only be increased when we compare the *Songs before Sunrise* with the *Giambi ed epodi* of Carducci which were written on identical subjects and during the same years. For Carducci, whose father had been imprisoned after 1831, whose intimate friends had suffered and even been executed for their connection with the Young Italy movement, might well have been excused had he shown some exaggeration of feeling, had his emotions led him into faults of literary excess. The dominant note of *Giambi ed epodi* is, however, one of fine restraint, of powerful concision, of sorrowing satire. The tone throughout is almost an undertone, broken only by some smothered cry of agony, some startling shout of herculean contempt, some sudden sigh of admiration or of love. Even the metre is virile, muscular, and self-controlled ; it does not intrude upon the attention or blur the understanding :

> Non fo madrigaletti
> Che voi mitriate d' immortalità.

This deeper feeling, this higher seriousness, this wider comprehension, give to Carducci's poems a strength and durability in comparison to which many of the *Songs before Sunrise* appear but as wind and air.   How damaging, for instance, is the contrast between the indiscriminate excitability of " The Eve of Revolution " and such wry wisdom as

> Accoglietemi, udite, O degli eroi
>   Esercito gentile :
> Triste novella io recherò fra voi :
>   La nostra patria è vile.

How infinitely more impressive, even than " On the Downs ", is the " Canto dell' amore ", or than all the turbulent invectives of Swinburne the final satirical reconciliation with Pio Nono, or the wide appeal addressed from Perugia :

> Salute, o genti umane affaticate !
> Tutto trapassa, e nullo può morir.
> Noi troppo odiammo e sofferimmo.   Amate :
> Il mondo è bello e santo è l' avvenir.

If, however, we may well regret that so large a proportion of the *Songs before Sunrise* are connected with the concrete problem of the *Risorgimento*, with which Swinburne with his falsetto muscularity was unfitted to deal, yet it is important that his failure in one section of his work should not blind us to his very real success in giving expression to those more inveterate experiences for which Young Italy was but the occasion and the symbol.   It is true, doubtless, that the politics of *Songs before Sunrise* are too shallow to awaken any lasting interest in the verses, and that the verses in their turn are too elaborate to allow of any consecutive interest in the politics.   But the moment Swinburne leaves the *Risorgimento* and Mazzini and sings of the theory of Liberty in the abstract, of Liberty and the Soul of Man, his poetry at once responds to the wider and fresher experience, its metrical beauty loses its purely narcotic quality, and communication is at last established.

The main weapon of those who would dismiss Swinburne as a mere prosodist is the criticism that " he lacked a central core ", that he was both morally and intellectually un-original in the sense that all his ideas and emotions were plainly literary, purely derivative. In saying this they not only confuse technique with value, but they overlook the fact that this central core, which burnt with a white ardour, is to be found in his love of Liberty. For him " Liberty " was a religion : something white and circumambient and intense. With it were fused all his childhood's experiences, the only experiences which he had undergone with any wholeness or intensity. The sea was part of it ; his successive heroes were also elements ; there entered into it the conflict between revolt and submission ; but the whole is greater than its parts : the whole comprises and explains the essential spiritual energy of Swinburne's being. His loathing of all restrictions, whether political, moral, intellectual, or social, amounted almost to claustrophobia : he was a white bird perpetually winged for escape ; he appeared to himself as some wild sea-mew beating against the bars. The defiance which is implicit in *Poems and Ballads* is to no slight extent to be explained as a gesture of liberation : the choruses of *Atalanta* echo the same unfailing struggle ; but it is in the more abstract poems of *Songs before Sunrise* that the accumulated energy of these passions shoots up in a steaming fountain of volcanic intensity.

In the first place, Liberty to him is the symbol of youth and health and light, the symbol of his highest

physical and spiritual enjoyments. It is for no merely
rhetorical purpose that he concludes his Epilogue with
the picture of a boy swimming on some June morning
out towards the sunrise; it is by no mere chance
that the epithets " bright ", " light ", " white ", flutter
around his Republic as they fluttered above the serene
head of Atalanta; it is with no unmeaning analogy that
his finer hymns end either in the thunder or the whisper
of the sea. Liberty is the faith that stands courageous
when " grey-haired hope " has fallen blind. She is the
eternal Truth :

> Because there is but one truth ;
>   Because there is but one banner ;
>   Because there is but one light ;
> Because we have with us our youth
>   Once, and one chance and one manner
>   Of service, and then the night.

Liberty is action and companionship, the hope of boyhood, the more serious faith of age ; she is pity and
she is love ; she is adventure and hatred ; she is the
" fair bare body of Wisdom " and she is the eternal
unreason ; she is the new dawn and yet she has for ever
existed ; she is the cause and the effect of all our human
energies and excitements. Liberty is then the Pantheon
of heroes :

> Yea, they are dead, men much more worth than thou ;
>   The savour of heroic lives that were,
>   Is it not mixed into thy common air ?
> The sense of them is shed about thee now :
>   Feel not thy brows a wind blowing from afar ?
>   Aches not thy forehead with a future star ?

She is " the cry of the world's heart's wrong " ; she is
the mother of men sad and triumphant ; she is the fierce
mistress of men, and she demands an ecstasy of sacrifice
and submission :

> I that have love and no more
>> Give you but love of you, sweet :
>>> He that hath more let him give ;
>> He that hath wings, let him soar :
>>> Mine is the heart at your feet
>>>> Here, that must love you to live.

Not only, however, did Swinburne see in Liberty the idealisation of his own temperament, not only do we recognise in the shining gestures of his Republican Virgin both the poignant cruelty of Dolores and the aloof gentleness of *Atalanta*, but an endeavour is made in the more important poems of *Songs before Sunrise* to give to this conception a far more universal meaning, to found thereon a whole philosophy of life. The thesis is indeed implicit throughout the volume, but it is more expressly stated in the three philosophic poems of " Genesis ", the " Hymn of Man ", and " Hertha ". The nucleus of Swinburne's theory is summarised by him in three effective stanzas of " A Year's Burden " :

> Are ye so strong, O kings, O strong men ?   Nay,
> Waste all ye will and gather all ye may,
> Yet one thing is there that ye shall not slay,
>> Even thought, that fire nor iron can affright.

> The woundless and invisible thought that goes
> Free throughout time as north or south wind blows,
> Far throughout space as east or west sea flows,
>> And all dark things before it are made bright.

> Thy thought, thy word, O soul republican,
> O spirit of life, O god whose name is man :
> What sea of sorrows but thy sight shall span ?

In the fierce invectives of " Before a Crucifix " Swinburne sings of the passing of the God of Churches, of the Jesus of the priests, and in " Christmas Antiphones " he again recurs to the theme, although in calmer tones :

> Man shall do for you,
>   Men the sons of man,
> What no God would do
> That they sought unto
>   While the blind years ran.

It is not, however, merely the God of the Churches whom he assails ; he attacks the very conception of a supreme deity. For what is this conception but an emanation of subjective sensibility, what is it but the timorous human desire to create an image of the Supreme Good as a relief and refuge from the presence of evil ? For what is death but " the shadow cast by life's wide wings ", and what is God but " the shade cast by the soul of man " ? In " Genesis " Swinburne endeavours to show how the conception of God was evolved by human fear, how this basic fallacy arose from a misunderstanding of the necessity, nay, even the identity, of good and evil :

> The immortal war of mortal things, that is
>   Labour and life and growth and good and ill,
> The mild antiphones that melt and kiss,
>   The violent symphonies that meet and kill,
>
> All nature of all things began to be,
>   But chiefest in the spirit (beast or man,
> Planet of heaven or blossom of earth or sea)
>   The divine contraries of life began.

God being thus the invention of man, it is man who remains the master : " Thou art judged, O judge, and the sentence has gone forth against thee, O God ", and " O fools," he cries, " he was God and is dead ". Or again :

> We men, the multiform features of man, whatsoever we be,
> Recreate him of whom we are creatures, and all we only
>   are he.

Not each man of all men is God, but God is the fruit of the
    whole ;
Indivisible spirit and blood, indiscernible body from soul.
Not men's but man's is the glory of godhead, the kingdom
    of time.

These destructive poems are effective for all their
rhetoric : here at least one feels Swinburne has grasped
a central conception which he follows with consistency,
and almost with concision. They become, however,
of even greater interest and importance when it is
recognised that they are but the preparation and background for " Hertha ", since this poem is perhaps
the best organised of all Swinburne's compositions.
Having disengaged with real lucidity and force the
central conception of " The great god Man, which is
God ", Swinburne proceeds to evolve his greater and
more intricate Trinity—the trinity of " Freedom, God,
and Man ". If man be greater than God, the soul of
man is greater than man, and the soul of man is
Liberty :

> Freedom we call it, for holier
> Name of the soul there is none.

The supremacy of this, the human over-soul, is based
upon no precedence and no domination ; it is coeval
with man ; it is at once objective and subjective ; it is
at once the master and the servant :

> I am that which began ;
>   Out of me the years roll ;
> Out of me God and man,
>   I am equal and whole ;
> God changes, and man, and the form of them bodily : I am
>   the soul.

> Before ever land was,
> Before ever the sea,

Or soft hair of the grass,
Or fair limbs of the tree,
Or•the flesh-coloured fruit of my branches, I was, and thy
soul was in me.

First life on my sources
First drifted and swam ;
Out of me are the forces
That save it or damn ;
Out of me man and woman, and wild-beast and bird ; before
God was, I am.

Beside or above me
Nought is there to go ;
Love or unlove me,
Unknow me or know ;
I am that which unloves me and loves : I am stricken, and I
am the blow.

The Goddess of Liberty demands no limitation of
human personality, she demands only the extension of
that personality, the fullest expression by each individual of his own possibilities. Thus only can truth
be obtained, thus only can the gift of life be justified :

For truth only is living,
Truth only is whole,
And the love of his giving
Man's polestar and pole :
Man, pulse of my centre, and fruit of my body, and seed of
my soul.

One birth of my bosom ;
One beam of mine eye ;
One topmost blossom
That scales the sky ;
Man, equal and one with me, man that is made of me, man
that is I.

It is impossible, after reading " Hertha ", not to
agree with Swinburne when he said, " Of all I have done,
I rate ' Hertha ' highest as a single piece, finding in it
the most of lyric force and music combined with the

most of condensed and clarified thought ".   Nor can
the clear white light of this, the most intense of his
poems, fail to illumine the whole of *Songs before Sunrise*,
and to justify the high claim of his own Epilogue :

> Not utterly struck spiritless
> For shame's sake and unworthiness
>   Of these poor forceless hands that come
>   Empty, these lips that should be dumb,
> This love whose seal can but impress
>   These weak word-offerings wearisome,
> Whose blessings have not strength to bless
>   Nor lightnings fire to burn up aught
>   Nor smite with thunders of their thought.
>
> One thought they have, even love ; one light,
> Truth, that keeps clear the sun by night ;
>   One chord, of faith as of a lyre ;
>   One heat, of hope as of a fire ;
> One heart, one music, and one might,
>   One flame, one altar, and one choir.

CHAPTER VIII

With the publication of *Songs before Sunrise* Swinburne bade farewell to what, in any other man, would have been a protracted adolescence, and entered into a period which, in some one else, would have been recognisable as that of middle age. The temperament of Swinburne does not, however, lend itself to such currently accepted chronology. He never fully experienced the emotions of adolescence ; he experienced only the evanescent emotions of puberty ; he never attained to that co-ordination of impulses which is the solace of middle age ; he attained only to a chaotic intensification of his pre-adult experiences. He had from childhood, we must repeat, been curiously impervious to any but a few isolated impressions ; after his thirty-fifth year this imperviousness spread like some callous growth across his receptivity. The original experiences, it is true, remained with undiminished intensity, and would often erupt with volcanic violence ; but they are wearyingly the same experiences, they are essentially the little stock in trade which he had acquired at Eton and at Balliol : they are not the impressions of a grown man. A mist of wastage, of fatuity, and of frustration thus begins to cling around his later poems, and our response to them is chilled. His fluency seems at moments to become redundance, his melody a jingle, his eloquence rhetoric, his enthusiasms appear but as some shrill and wearisome iteration. The hero-worship which meant so much to him loses its quality of boyish loyalty and strikes us as foolish and undiscriminating. Even that high revolt which was the mainspring of his genius becomes something merely mutinous, something irritatingly ill-behaved.

If such depressing reactions are not unduly to colour our appreciation of the fine body of poetry which he produced after 1871, and even after 1879, it is of importance thus to isolate their effect. For if people would approach Swinburne with the realisation that in his early work he was a poet of amazing promise, and that in his later work he was a great man of letters, there would be less danger of their confusing the one period with the other, or of their attributing a false importance to the fact that his poetry is largely derivative, being founded on literature rather than on life. This familiar theory is but half a truth, and ignores the central phenomenon of Swinburne's genius, the strange pathological circumstance of his partially arrested development. For from this aspect Swinburne was, and remains, eternally immature, and his poetry suffers thereby, not in the direction of invalidity, decidedly not in that of insincerity, but in a certain stellar detachment, a certain aloofness from ordinary human experience, which obstructs communication.

There is evidence to show that this curious repetitive quality in Swinburne's genius, and the vague disappointment which it engenders, had begun by this year 1871 to disturb, and even to alienate, his Oxford contemporaries and his early Pre-Raphaelite friends. Meredith, who had always been somewhat disconcerted by the patrician misbehaviour of Swinburne, decided definitely that the man lacked " central core ". Rossetti, who by then was already surrendering to misanthropy, if not to chloral, finally abandoned all hope of bringing the little bloke into direct contact with practical life. To him, moreover, in his hatred of politics in general and Italian politics in particular, even the *Songs before Sunrise* must have appeared a very meaningless digression. On Burne-Jones the schoolboy prurience of Swinburne's letters may well have grated as being, by that date, scarcely necessary. And to Morris, exuberant, bustling, practical, the lack of obvious purpose in Swinburne's poetry became a veritable barrier against appreciation. " But to confess and be hanged," he wrote later, " you know I never could really sympathise with Swinburne's work ; it always seemed to me to be founded on literature and not on Nature. . . . The surroundings of life are so stern and unplayful that nothing can take hold of people which is not rooted in deepest reality and is quite at first hand." Of course there was Jowett, absorbingly tactful, so softly authoritative, so masterfully mundane : there would be holidays with reading-parties at Pitlochry, and there would be visits to Balliol when Mrs. Knight, the housekeeper, would remove the bottles from Mr. Swinburne's luggage, and when Jowett would rescue him on Sunday afternoons from the dangerous precincts of Brasenose, from the deleterious companionship of Walter Pater. " I am happy ", wrote Swinburne after one of such visits, " to note a steady progress in the University of sound and thorough republican feeling among the younger

fellows of colleges as well as the undergraduates."
But such excursions were mere interludes in a life of
increasing monotony and loneliness. The eight years
from 1871 to 1879 lend themselves to no detailed
treatment. The circumstances of his outward life
continued almost unchanged. He could still be seen
drifting along Holborn in his neat little suit, almost
somnambulistic in his detachment from the whirl
around him. He could still be seen sitting very erect
at the London Restaurant in Chancery Lane eating
asparagus slowly, vacantly, but with peculiar distinction.
The legends of his solitary drinking bouts in his rooms
in Great James Street were not exaggerated, and, as
before, he would be rescued periodically by his relations
and return after a few weeks to London, plump, sunburnt, but still somnambulistic. There were the same
flickering gestures, the same strident crescendo when
aroused, the same abstracted indifference to all that
fell outside his own restricted circle of interests. To
the old idolatries, to the old hatreds, he would respond
with the familiar jet of scalding eloquence ; but from
every new stimulus from the wide new movements of
life and art and politics, he remained passively but not
discourteously aloof. Vaguely he was conscious that
he was losing touch with his own external existence.
He would sit for hours by the fire, his toes turned
inwards, his hands meeting in a curious attitude of
penitence. From time to time a friend would sit with
him " cherchant pourquoi il voulait tant s'évader de la
réalité ". And with dusk would come melancholia,
the consciousness of what he called " the chill monotonous puppet-show of my life " : the knowledge of how
the night would end. And thus gradually the fierce

red aureole of Pre-Raphaelite days faded into a dun and sandy mane.

It must be noted also that these dimly apprehended discomfitures produced in Swinburne moods of deep depression, alternating with moods of arrogant violence —moods almost of persecution mania. He went out of his way to pick a quarrel with Emerson in circumstances which constitute perhaps the most entertaining of Sir Edmund Gosse's many reminiscences. He came to imagine for some recondite reason that George Eliot was " hounding on her myrmidons to his destruction ". He embarked on a lively but not unembittered controversy with Furnivall and the Shakspeare Society, a controversy which ran a somewhat scurrilous course for fourteen years. Such activities represent merely a phase, or perhaps an angle, of his character which became unduly prominent between the ages of thirty-two and forty-two, and they should not be allowed to blur either the portrait of the garish and passionately loyal mutineer of Balliol, or that of the courteous and kindly scholar of No. 2 The Pines. Nor were the dark clouds which hang over this period entirely unrelieved by gleams of sunshine. It might be true that his older friends regarded his literary development with ill-concealed disappointment, but outside this narrower radius his popularity was increasing in ever-widening circles, and a younger generation was arising who hailed him as the Messiah of a new poetic age. Even in his retirement, even at 3 Great James Street, the lapping of this rising tide would reach him, and it is with a touch, a pleasing touch, of conscious under-statement that he could write in 1872, " and surely my name must be worth something in the market ".

His name, the name of Swinburne, in the early 'seventies ! How can we recapture the faith and fire which it then aroused ? A flaming symbol of emancipation, the very wine of freedom, the zest of heresy, the whole music of passion ; a group of fevered undergraduates swaying arm in arm together along the Turl chanting the stanzas of " Dolores " ; a young man alone pacing a room in London intoning " Anactoria " to the early dawn ; the surreptitious ferment in those English homes from which the books were banned ; the wide adventure and the wider hope ; the excitement of discovery ; the sharp throb of youth.

The position which he had thus come to occupy in the thoughts of the younger generation brought him at this period the friendship of two men, different in calibre from those with whom he had hitherto been acquainted, widely, and indeed singularly, different from each other. The first was Edmund Gosse, whom he met in January 1871, and with whom, after some slight hesitation due to diffidence on both sides, he formed an enduring and very stimulating intimacy. The second was Walter Theodore Watts. Mr. Watts, who, in 1896, assumed the additional surname of Dunton, did not, in any sense, belong to the younger generation. In fact, he was Swinburne's senior by some five years. Nor can the ill-success of his early overtures to the poet be ascribed to diffidence. In literary matters Walter Watts was a late-flowering though hardy plant : it was not until the age of forty that, under the aegis of Doctor Hake, he bustled into literary society : it was not till he was sixty-six that he published *Aylwin*—a novel which gave him at the time a considerable reputation. There can be no doubt of

L

the sincerity of Watts's passion for literature in general, and for literary celebrities in particular. " My life ", he recorded later, " has always been singularly exposed to beautiful influences." During these earlier years when he was working as a solicitor at St. Ives he had flung himself with rare pertinacity into the pursuit and capture of George Borrow, tracking down that cantankerous quarry upon Wimbledon Common, splashing round him in the surf at Whitby. To Borrow had succeeded Rossetti, whose financial affairs had by then been seriously complicated owing to the vagaries of Howell. A similar cause first brought him into connection with Swinburne, to whom he was recommended towards the end of 1872. It was not, however, till the following year that Swinburne definitely decided to place his affairs in the hands of Walter Watts. The purely business connection thus established appears quite rapidly to have developed into friendship. Already by December 1873 Watts had become " a legal friend whom perhaps you know ", and by 1875 we find the two spending the first of many summer holidays together, at Southwold, this time, on the Suffolk coast. It must have been during this sojourn that Swinburne in his turn established over Watts the " beautiful influence " which the latter was so quick to acknowledge and to foster. In January of the new year this influence is already apparent : we find Watts writing to his idol with all the fussy kindliness of the Putney period :

I took the poem to Maccoll who has accepted it for £20 for the *Athenæum*. I am to meet him in town about the other poems you left with me, one of which I shall offer him. . . . Do not, pray, forget that I am to have the manuscript

of *Erechtheus*. Where is it ? The manuscript, too, of the
present poems I understand you to have promised me—
n'est-ce pas ?

Nor was Swinburne himself insensible to the
disinterested devotion of this " hero of friendship ".
Even in 1877 we find his letters beginning " As my
friend Watts knows . . ." and ending " . . . and Watts
also was most strongly of the same mind ". It will be
safe, therefore, to date the " beautiful influence " from
July 1876.

Against the background thus disclosed, the work
accomplished or essayed by Swinburne between the
years 1871 and 1879 stands out in marmoreal splendour.
Apart from the literary articles which he contributed
to the *Fortnightly Review* and which have since been
included among the collected edition of his works, he
completed and published the stupendous mass of
Bothwell in 1874, and *George Chapman* in the same
year. In 1875 appeared *Erechtheus*, and three years
later was issued the second series of *Poems and Ballads*.
Tristram of Lyonesse, which had been begun at Pitlochry
in August of 1871, was constantly in hand during the
years that followed, while such poems as the " Forsaken
Garden ", " The Garden of Cymodoce ", as well as the
several translations from Villon, all date from before
1877. His most exhaustive occupation, however,
during these eight years, or at any rate after 1874, when
he had rid himself of the vast incubus of *Bothwell*, was
a new and even more intensive study of Aeschylus, of
Shakespeare, and of the Elizabethan and Jacobean
dramatists. He contemplated at one moment a work
in two volumes dealing with the age of Shakespeare,
and he actually planned an extensive monograph upon

the metrical development of Shakespeare's verse. His first sketch of such an examination appeared in the *Fortnightly* for May 1875, and the criticism which it provoked from the experts so discouraged him that he abandoned his original intention. But he emerged from these studies with an even profounder knowledge of his subject, and remained thereafter a distinguished scholar in such matters and a widely recognised specialist.

Meanwhile the main landmarks of this period are *Bothwell, Erechtheus*, and the second series of *Poems and Ballads*. The five acts of *Bothwell*, which between them represent upwards of six hundred closely printed pages, had taken Swinburne over three years to complete. Begun in 1871, the play had been finished in March of 1874 and was published in June of that year. It was greeted with general, if somewhat mild approval, and even to-day we cannot but regard it, even the outside of it, with anything but awe-struck respect. It is permissible to suppose that Swinburne had meant to write a trilogy on Mary Queen of Scots, keeping the two later plays within the limits and in the note of *Chastelard*, the last line of which was clearly intended to mark the transition. He approached the work with zest and fluency, being convinced, as he wrote to Clarence Stedman, that " the fusion of lyric with dramatic form gives the highest type of poetry ". But as he progressed, the scholar and the student in him encroached upon the poet : his gift of composition, never a very sturdy element in his genius, collapsed completely under the accumulating weight of material ; his fine intellectual honesty forbade the taking of short cuts or the suppression of unaccommodating factors ; his

abiding insensitiveness to his audience failed to warn
him that the play was becoming intolerably dull ; his
very fluency led him, as always, into being diffuse, and
the result, in the words of Edward Thomas, is " a
monstrous achievement, the most solemn proof existing
of Swinburne's power of fundamental brain work ".
Swinburne himself appears in the end to have had some
qualms about *Bothwell*. It is true that a few months
after its publication he interviewed Henry Irving in the
hope of seeing it produced on the stage, and was somewhat surprised to find that " Irving's mood was
taciturn". On the other hand, whereas in his dedication to Victor Hugo he had called it " mon drame
épique ", yet he later changed this appellation to " my
chronicle play ", and he finally described the drama
merely as an " ambitious, conscientious, comprehensive
piece of work "; which indeed it is. For in truth
Bothwell is not an epic, nor yet a drama, nor even a
romance. It is too poetic for narrative, and too
historical for poetry : it lacks concentration and outline. The central and consistent theme is neither love,
nor crime, nor character : again and again the central
theme becomes politics—a subject into which Swinburne in the best of circumstances had no devouring
insight, a subject essentially so centrifugal that it requires the firmest handling if ever it is to be moulded
into a work of art. It is in this very firmness of handling that Swinburne has failed. There are of course
many excellent and beautiful passages in *Bothwell* : the
French and English songs and lyrics are, as always,
perfectly conceived and executed ; there is the fine tirade
of John Knox in Act IV., the skilful character analysis
embodied in the conflict between Darnley and the

Queen in Act II. There are passages in which the
passionate self-abandonment with which the Queen
surrenders herself to Bothwell is treated with a wild
magnificence :

> I would I had on breast or hand or brow
> In crown or clasp the whole gold wrought of the earth,
> In one keen jewel the store of all the sea,
> That I might throw down at your hand or foot,
> Sea, land, and all that in them is of price,
> Or in the strong wine of my piercing love
> Melt the sole pearl of the earth, and drink dissolved
> The cost of all the world's work.

The interpretation of character, although intermittent, is at moments extremely vivid and arresting.
The whole of Darnley lives in one sudden outburst of
the Queen :

> With his lewd eyes and sodden sidelong face.

And in one passage at least we catch the essence of
Swinburne's obsession for Mary's character :

> My soul
> Is a wave too that springs against the light
> And beats and bursts with one great strain of joy
> As the sea breaking.

But for all this, and in spite of the high level of
technical excellence maintained throughout, the reading
of *Bothwell* is, it must be confessed, an irksome business,
bringing with it a sense of depression that such a wealth
of talent, so vast a store of energy and erudition, should
have been expended upon a work so long, so unprofit-
able, and so inconclusive.

It is almost with relief that we turn from the tangled
maze of *Bothwell* to the clear-cut symmetry of *Erechtheus.* For this, the second of Swinburne's hellenic
dramas, is, as Sir Edmund Gosse has pointed out, the

most organic of all his works.   It may be surmised that
Swinburne, who possessed all the scholar's sensitiveness to any slur upon his scholarship, had been unduly
impressed by those criticisms which had accused *Atalanta* of being unhellenic in spirit, and that he determined to prove, by composing at least one play of
unassailable attic exactitude, that whatever liberties had
in the former play been taken with the hellenic method,
had been taken deliberately and not in ignorance.   It
was at Pitlochry, and under Jowett's eye, that he
embarked upon an intensive study of Aeschylus, and
it was thus when the Aeschylean manner had been
thoroughly absorbed and digested, when the disturbing
romanticism of Bothwell had been for the moment
worked out of his system, and after another visit to
Jowett at Malvern, that he retired quietly to lodgings
at Wragford near Southwold in Suffolk, and completed
the whole of *Erechtheus* quickly, calmly, and without
interruption.

" It can scarcely be denied ", writes Sir Edmund
Gosse, " that in the general conduct of this tragedy he
rises, in our altitude of moral emotion that he reaches
nowhere else, to an atmosphere which few modern
poets have even attempted to breathe."   I have experienced some difficulty in sharing Sir Edmund Gosse's
enthusiasm.   For on first reading the play appears too
deliberately Aeschylean ; the elevation which it undoubtedly attains impresses one, not as the inevitable
widening of an emotion unconsciously released, but
as the artificial selection of a rarefied atmosphere, as
the conscious adoption of an empyrean plane.   This
impression is increased by the rigid subordination of
human personality and endeavour to the inscrutable

whims of destiny; for although heroism is the theme of the tragedy, yet the heroism displayed is too purposeless, too inhuman, to stir our modern sensibility. In *Atalanta* also the fates had played their part with ruthless stupidity, but the final catastrophe had at least been precipitated by the human emotions of love and jealousy. In *Erechtheus* it is the gods alone who in their petty cruelty evolve the tragedy, the uttermost expenditure of human sacrifice and virtue being but of incidental avail. It cannot be denied, of course, that the latter tragedy in its grim bare outlines is more classically hellenic than is the tremulous shimmer of *Atalanta*, or that, if regarded merely as a literary *pastiche*, *Erechtheus* is the more scholarly achievement. But if we are to reckon his play among the masterpieces of Swinburne, we need surely to feel that something more than his skill and erudition were engaged, that some wider experience inspires its " marmoreal uniformity of diction ". In seeking for this central theme we shall be disconcerned by the deliberate archaism of language, an archaism which recalls too persistently the early Aeschylus, and which is not, as in *Atalanta*, rigidly subordinated to the dominant key in which the melody is tuned. A further difficulty is the lack of concentration in the dramatic interest of the story; it is never wholly clear whether Athens is to be destroyed by the Thracians or by the sea; it is never wholly clear whether the central theme is the sacrifice of Chthonia, or the heroism of her mother; and the final holocaust of Erechtheus and his remaining daughters is treated in a manner wholly unconvincing and almost incidental.

If therefore we approach *Erechtheus* hoping to find therein either an intense dramatic concentration, a convincing human interest, a conflict of pity and terror, or even the amazing imagery of *Atalanta*, we shall achieve only a deep respect for its high competence as a literary reconstruction, coupled with a useful realisation that Swinburne could, in certain circumstances, write with cool and impersonal concision. But if we approach this play in the mood of *Songs before Sunrise* and regard it primarily as an evocation of the ideal human Republic, as a picture of the unhesitating sacrifices which idealised human nature should make to the conception of corporate freedom, then we shall be able to identify its inspiration with the central fire of Swinburne's conviction ; we shall be able to appreciate the rare restraint with which for once this passionate conviction is conveyed ; and the bleached marble of its austerity will pulsate for us like mellowed amber in the sun :

From the depths of the springs of my spirit a fountain is
    poured of thanksgiving,
            My country, my mother, for thee,
That thy dead for their death shall have life in thy sight
    and a name ever living
            At heart of thy people to be.
In the darkness of change on the waters of time they shall
    turn from afar
To the beam of this dawn for a beacon, the light of these
    pyres for a star.
They shall see thee who love and take comfort, who hate
    thee shall see and take warning,
            Our Mother that makest us free ;
And the sons of thine earth shall have help of the Waves
    that made war on their morning,
            And friendship and fame of the sea.

With the year 1878 Swinburne's constitution finally collapsed under the strain to which it had for so long been exposed. It was in January of that year that he

spent a last " boisterous month " with John Nichol at
Glasgow : a final Saturnalia. By May he was too ill
and dispirited to accept an invitation from Victor Hugo
to attend the centenary celebrations in honour of
Voltaire. The winter of that year witnessed a further
decline, and Sir Edmund Gosse describes him as being
" worn and feeble, sometimes tottering like an old man,
and glad to accept a hand to help him up and down
stairs ". The early summer of 1879 was passed at
Holmwood, but in July he returned to London and to
his new rooms at 25 Guildford Street, Russell Square.
Here again he succumbed to brandy, and in the early
weeks of September he was assailed by acute alcoholic
dysentery which brought him to the verge of a squalid
and disreputable death. It was at this moment that
Watts-Dunton arrived in a four-wheeler and translated
the dying poet to Putney. Swinburne survived. He
survived for thirty further years as a placid man of
letters, a little wistful, perhaps, at moments, a little
stouter as the years rolled by, but to the end scholarly,
and courteous to the end. Watts was justly triumphant :
he had saved the life of one of England's greatest poets ;
and for himself and his two sisters he had secured a
residence, which might well become historical, and
which in any case was desirable and semi-detached.
Lady Jane Swinburne with relief and gratitude paid
the expenses of their installation.

Before abandoning his independent existence Swinburne had fortunately given to the world a collection
of poems which to many of his more intelligent
admirers represents the most durable monument of
his lyrical genius. *Poems and Ballads : Second Series*
was published in June 1878, but most of the poems it

contains had been composed long previously, and Sir
Edmund Gosse records, in fact, that almost half the
whole collection had been completed by the autumn
of 1876. There are, of course, many pieces in this
volume which are mainly of an incidental or technical
interest. There are several translations from the
French, eleven from Villon and one from Victor Hugo,
which serve merely to illustrate his unrivalled skill in
this form of literary activity. His scholarship is
represented by two poems in Latin and three in French,
while among the purely metrical exercises I should
include not only " Choriambics " and " Triads " but
also the unsuccessful " Song in Season ", the " Sestina ",
and the double Sestina entitled " The Complaint of
Lisa ". " A Wasted Vigil " might also fall within this
category, since it represents an obvious experiment in
the changes which can be rung on the Omar Khayyám
quatrain, but there are phrases in this poem which
suggest a more personal experience and which lift the
quatrains above the level of mere experiment :

> Last year, a brief while since, an age ago,
> A whole year past, with bud and bloom and snow,
> O moon that wast in heaven, what friends were we !
>   Couldst thou not watch with me ?
>
> Old moons and last year's flowers, and last year's snows !
> Who now saith to thee, moon ? or who saith, rose ?
> O dust and ashes, once found fair to see !
>   Couldst thou not watch with me ?

Of the *Songs before Sunrise* we have an echo, not
only in the " Ode to Kossuth " and in " Rizpah ", but
also in that curious poem " The White Czar " (1877),
in which we detect for the first time a note of bourgeois
jingoism, an unmistakable note of Theodore Watts.
A more important reversion to the spirit of *Songs before*

Sunrise will be found in " The Last Oracle ", a Delphic hymn on the theme of " Vicisti Galilee ", a beautiful and melodious poem but one that lacks direction. A pleasant tone is, moreover, given to the volume by the introduction of a series of personal verses, urbane, complimentary, or elegiac. The charming dedication to Sir R. Burton is as felicitous as the analogous compliments addressed by Tennyson to FitzGerald and F. D. Maurice. There are several admirable poems on literary subjects, such as the Sonnet to Cyril Tourneur, the verses to Victor Hugo, the fine tribute to Marlowe entitled " In the Bay ", and the justly famous " Ballad of François Villon ". The minor elegiacs also, such as the " Epicede " to James Graham, the " Inferiae " to his own father, the verses to Barry Cornwall, and the " Birth Song " in memory of Oliver Madox Brown, are welcome as illustrating his affectionate loyalty to his friends, a side of his nature which has too often been obscured by the fumes and thunder of less intimate idolatries and antagonisms. And finally, among the secondary qualities of this volume, should be noted those descriptive poems of a softly modulated sensuousness, such as "A Ballad of Dreamland ", " Four Songs of Four Seasons ", and the less successful " The Year of the Rose ".

I have reserved for the end my examination of the seven outstanding poems which give to the volume of 1878 so distinctive a place in Swinburne's literary development, and which in themselves represent the highest level of his achievement. For in truth these poems stand midway between his mutinous puberty and the staid and studious quiescence in which he became thereafter enveloped. The landscape is the

same, but it is softening to the more mellow lights
of afternoon ; a certain tremulous lethargy, a certain
frightened wistfulness, has stolen on his music ; a sigh
of valediction is stirring in the woods ; the cymbals
have been abandoned for the flute.   Even in " At a
Month's End ", the most passionate of this series, which
might be said to bear

> The print and perfume of old passion,
>   The wild-beast mark of panther's fangs,

there is a note of saddened acquiescence, a note of
resignation and farewell no less poignant than the
embittered repudiations of " The Triumph of Time " :

> Silent we went an hour together,
>   Under grey skies by waters white.
> Our hearts were full of windy weather,
>   Clouds and blown stars and broken light.
>
> Full of cold clouds and moonbeams drifted
>   And streaming storms and straying fires,
> Our souls in us were stirred and shifted
>   By doubts and dreams and foiled desires.
>
> Across, aslant, a scudding sea-mew
>   Swam, dipped and dropped, and grazed the sea ;
> And one with me I could not dream you ;
>   And one with you I could not be.

"At Parting " also, in spite of its jaunty anapaests,
ends with a similar valedictory dismissal, while in the
beautiful conclusion of " A Vision of Spring in Winter "
we catch the perfect cadence of a great poet's farewell
to his own boyhood :

> . . . The sweet swift eyes and songs of hours that were ;
> These may'st thou not give back for ever ; these,
>   As at the sea's heart all her wrecks lie waste,
>   Lie deeper than the sea ;

> But flowers thou may'st, and winds, and hours of ease,
>   And all its April to the world thou may'st
>   Give back, and half my April back to me.

In " Ex-voto " his worship of the sea is mingled with thoughts of death, whereas the whole theme of " A Forsaken Garden " is the mutability of human affections, the erosion of time, the final inrush of a greater annihilation when even death shall be annihilated. More essentially lyrical, since it arises from a direct personal impression, expands to general human experience and retracts again to the intimate, is the short poem entitled " Relics "—to my mind the most perfect because the most subtle of all Swinburne's lesser melodies. For in this outstanding poem, in this evocation from " the world of the unapparent dead ", Swinburne has given to the FitzGerald metre an indefinitely plangent cadence, a symbolic wistfulness vibrating far beyond the meaning or even the music of the words themselves :

> Out of the hard green wall of leaves that clomb
> They showed like windfalls of the snow-soft foam,
>   Or feathers from the weary south-wind's wing,
> Fair as the spray that it came shoreward from.
>
> .   .   .   .   .   .
>
> Of days more sweet than thou wast sweet to smell,
> Of flower-soft thoughts that came to flower and fell,
>   Of loves that lived a lily's life and died,
> Of dreams now dwelling where dead roses dwell.

And then, of course, there is the " Ave atque Vale ", a poem which at one time Swinburne had decided to destroy. For it had been written in April 1867 under the shock of what subsequently proved to be a false report of the death of Baudelaire in Brussels, and his irritation at this fortuitous solecism appears to have prejudiced the poet against what is universally regarded

as his greatest elegiac achievement. In a sense, of
course, this poem also is derivative and literary : there
are echoes of Moschus, echoes of Milton and Shelley,
unmistakable echoes of Catullus. But the emotion is
pervading and sincere ; and as Mr. Edward Thomas
has pointed out in his admirable analysis of this poem,
the treatment, within the limits of the elegiac con-
vention, is original.

Swinburne pictures himself as standing under " the
veiled porches of the Muse funereal ", actually beside
the bier of the dead poet. This almost physical contact
throws over the lines a bitter breath of the macabre,
gives to them a chilling throb of awe. For this is no
Christian ritual which he is celebrating, but rather some
despairing Pagan libation, and the salt courageous
savour of Roman pessimism gives to the lines that
astringent quality which is the secret of their appro-
priateness and of their strength :

> There is no help for these things ; none to mend
> And none to mar ; not all our songs, O friend,
> Will make death clear or make life durable.
> Howbeit with rose and ivy and wild vine
> And with wild notes about this dust of thine
> At least I fill the place where white dreams dwell
> And wreathe an unseen shrine.
>
> .   .   .   .   .
>
> For thee, O now a silent soul, my brother,
> Take at my hands this garland, and farewell.
> Thin is the leaf, and chill the wintry smell,
> And chill the solemn earth, a fatal mother,
> With sadder than the Niobean womb,
> And in the hollow of her breasts a tomb.
> Content thee, howsoe'er, whose days are done ;
> There lies not any troublous thing before,
> Nor sight nor sound to war against thee more,
> For whom all winds are quiet as the sun,
> All waters as the shore.

CHAPTER IX

NO. 2 THE PINES, 1879–1909

I HAVE often striven to think with greater kindliness of Watts-Dunton—ascribing to arrant snobbishness my own resentment at his bland self-satisfaction, his suburban complacency. Nor have I any sympathy with those who contend that Swinburne had better have died in 1879. The facts are patent. Swinburne had lost his health, his self-control, his dignity almost, certainly his zest in life : he was losing even, a more pitiable De Musset, the pride in his own genius. Watts rescued and redeemed. There were thirty years of useful suburban study. Why cavil at so salutary a redemption ?

One could leave it all at that, were it not for the great bulk of work produced at Putney, were it not that Swinburne himself, under the stimulus of Watts, inclined in later years to prefer his post-redemption verses to the poetry of his younger age. It becomes legitimate, therefore, to indicate the nature of Watts's influence, and to suggest why the waning fires of middle age were further damped and smothered by the brown blankets of No. 2 The Pines. The rôle of redeemer is one which, in the most spiritual circumstances, requires a marked delicacy of execution. Watts was wary; he

160

was capable, he was shrewd, he was always there; his patience was highly commendable, his pertinacity inspires awe. He possessed a will of iron, which he exercised without the appearance, and certainly without the consciousness, of cruelty. His solicitude for Swinburne's health was wholly admirable; his solicitude for Swinburne's manuscripts is almost touching. In business matters he was efficient, a little high-handed, but perfectly honest: even from the material point of view his redemption of Swinburne proved a highly paying concern. But from the first he allowed a certain proprietary flavour to vulgarise the manner of this redemption, and as the years wore on he inclined to strut somewhat, frock-coated and complacent, with wide self-embracing gestures as of some lion-tamer in the ring. His one fault, if Watts-Dunton had a fault, was jealousy, the arrogant, self-assertive form of jealousy which echoes in his boast: " From this moment (1879) Swinburne's connection with Bohemian London ceased entirely ". Nor was this jealousy confined to those of Swinburne's older friends, who might with some justice be described as deleterious: Watts was jealous of every pre-redemption influence; he was jealous of all Swinburne's most essential experiences; he was jealous of his boyhood, jealous of Northumberland, jealous of Eton, acutely jealous of *Poems and Ballads*. It was under Watts's influence that Swinburne attacked Whistler, that he repudiated Baudelaire and Walt Whitman, and that in the final years he committed the most distressing of all apostasies, those jingo *Songs after Sunset*, in which he attacked the Home Rule movement and welcomed the South African War. It is not surprising that such

M

a caging of the " light white seamew " should provoke resentment.

Let us not, however, allow this resentment to blind us to the very real qualities of Watts's character. Let us try to think of him, as Mr. Beerbohm thinks of him, as " a nice old codger " (I am quoting Mr. Beerbohm), as " a deeply emotional human being whose appeal was as much to the heart as to the head ", as a " rich nature ", as something " shaggy and old and chubby " (I am quoting from " No. 2 The Pines "). His passion for literature was of unassailable sincerity ; his novel *Alwyn* is a fine if lengthy piece of work, through which runs an impressive vein of mysticism, a curious repudiation of the genteel ; the reviews which he published in the *Athenæum* show him to have been a man of wide reading and possessed of a sound, if somewhat conventional, critical faculty. As a companion to Swinburne, as a touchstone for the latter's erudition, no one could have been more convenient. Nor can we doubt that the poet regarded his friend, " this pearl most perfect found in all the sea ", with real gratitude, with real affection, and with real respect. It was only when Watts assumed the Lavengro pose that Swinburne jibbed. " The almost adoring expression ", writes Mrs. Watts-Dunton (a young lady to whom Watts was married in 1905), " which came into Swinburne's eyes when he looked at Walter made me realise how deeply and gratefully conscious he was of the incalculable blessing the magnetic presence of his friend had been to him all the happy years he had spent under his roof." The roof, incidentally, was mainly, if not wholly, Swinburne's ; nor am I certain that " magnetic ", in spite of its impression of adhesiveness,

is exactly the epithet which applies.   But we may leave
it at that.

For the rest, there is but little more to be said of
Swinburne's biography.   The routine of his life was
early prescribed for him, nor was the prescription
altered in the thirty years that followed.   He rose at
10 A.M; at 11 he took his walk ; at 1 he returned ; at
1.30 he had luncheon ; from 2.30 to 4.30 he rested in
his bedroom ; from 4.30 to 6.30 he worked in his study ;
from 6.30 to 7.50 he read Dickens to Walter in the
drawing-room ; at 8 he dined ; at 9 he returned to his
study, where he worked till midnight.   His windows
looked out into the back garden.   Across the little strip
of grass a statue, late of Cheyne Walk, shimmered
against the privet; there were trees beyond, and a few
irises and geraniums against the ivy.   His personal
possessions were grouped around him—his books, the
Empire chairs, the serpentine candlesticks, the engrav-
ings of ships and storms at sea, the little statuette of
Victor Hugo, the print of Ben Jonson.   Above his
writing-table the acetylene gas hissed gently.   " Here
I am," he wrote to Lord Houghton, " like Mr. Tennyson at Faringford, close to the edge of a noble down."
Swinburne, as we have seen, had never been very
sensitive to his immediate surroundings.

His health was quickly restored : Watts saw to it
that there should be no further relapse.   " I never ",
he wrote in December 1879, " was fresher or stronger
or happier at twenty than now and for many weeks
back."   In 1882 there occurred an excitement : he
was invited to Paris by Hugo to attend the jubilee of
Le Roi s'amuse.   Watts went too.   They stayed in a
hotel together, and Watts had toothache, and Swinburne

dined alone with Victor Hugo. It was not a successful dinner. " Je suis heureux ", said Victor Hugo, " de vous serrer la main comme à un fils." But to the cataract of Swinburne's adulation, to the full flood of his correct but very English French, the old man could only murmur, " Mais qu'est-ce qu'il me raconte là ? Qu'est-ce qu'il me raconte ? " " After dinner ", Swinburne wrote to his mother, " he drank my health in a little speech of which, though I sat just opposite him, my accursed deafness prevented my hearing a single word." To this speech Swinburne replied, draining his glass in honour of his distinguished host, and in true Border fashion breaking the glass behind him when the toast was drunk. By which gesture the Master was very seriously annoyed.

And the years passed, and with their passage the " scarlet and azure macaw " of 1866 shaded off into the " book-monk of a suburban Thebaïs ". The death of Victor Hugo in 1885 came as a deep affliction ; the death of Lady Jane Swinburne in 1896 overwhelmed him with grief. " From this moment ", if I may again quote Sir Edmund Gosse," he became even more gentle, more remote, more unupbraiding than ever. He went on gliding over the commons of Wimbledon with the old noiseless regularity, but it could hardly be said that he held a place any longer in the ordinary world around him. The thirteen last years of Swinburne's life were spent almost as if within a Leyden jar."

The vast bulk of material which Swinburne published between the years 1879 and 1909 is liable, if treated indiscriminately, to do some harm to his final reputation, and requires therefore somewhat drastic sifting. The unfortunate circumstance that the technique of these later productions is at least as excellent as that of his early compositions, whereas the fine wild spirit which informed his earlier work has disappeared, accounts predominantly for the present reaction against Swinburne, and for the fact that so many people, with some justification, find him dull. Nor would I hesitate to affirm that Swinburne should be read only in selections, provided, of course, that the selections are not those chosen and published by Watts. It will be best perhaps to begin by a catalogue of the works actually published within this period :

1880. Songs of the Springtides.
1880. A Study of Shakespeare.
1880. Studies in Song.
1880. Heptalogia.
1881. Mary Stuart.
1882. Tristram of Lyonesse.
1883. A Century of Roundels.
1884. A Midsummer Holiday.
1885. Marino Faliero.
1886. Miscellanies.
1886. A Study of Victor Hugo.
1887. Locrine.
1889. A Study of Ben Jonson.
1889. Poems and Ballads : Third Series.
1892. The Sisters.
1894. Astrophel.
1894. Studies in Prose and Poetry.
1896. The Tale of Balen.
1899. Rosamund, Queen of the Lombards.
1904. A Channel Passage, and other Poems.
1905. Love's Cross-currents.
1908. The Duke of Gandia.
1908. The Age of Shakespeare.

In addition to these twenty-three volumes the following posthumous works were also published :

1909. Three Plays of Shakespeare. (Harper Bros.)
1909. Shakespeare. (Henry Frowde.)
1913. Charles Dickens. (Chatto & Windus.)
1917. Posthumous Poems. (Heinemann.)
1919. Contemporaries of Shakespeare. (Heinemann.)

Nor can all mention be omitted of the manuscripts which Mr. Wise purchased from Watts, although the great majority date prior to 1879. Seventy or eighty of these have been privately printed by Mr. Wise, and copies thereof deposited in the British Museum. They remain there for the perusal of the student.

Of this formidable, and in fact overwhelming, array of volumes eleven can be deferred for more general examination in the chapter dealing with Swinburne as a critic and a writer of prose ; six represent plays ; the remaining eleven, I fear, are in verse. It would be beyond the scope of this monograph to enter into any very detailed examination of all that Swinburne composed after 1879 ; nor would it square with my own intention to cloy the interest which I feel, and which I trust I have conveyed, in his earlier verse by discussing at any length the merits and defects of the twenty-eight volumes which have above been catalogued. It must be admitted, moreover, that the continuous reading even of those eleven volumes of poetry is apt to become a weariness to the flesh, an ordeal which can only be surmounted by those gifted with an actual passion for the technique of prosody. To the ordinary reader the vast bulk and uniformity of Swinburne's later verse is apt, unless care is taken, to destroy all zest for what is really important in his work, since the whole business, in appearance at least, is so very much the same.

Such a warning is necessary even in regard to *Songs*

of the Springtides, although two of the four long poems
it contains were certainly composed before 1879.
" The Garden of Cymodoce " celebrates the Island of
Sark, which he had visited with John Nichol in the
spring of 1876 : there can be no question of Swinburne's
enthusiasm for that island, or of the intense pleasure
which he had that May derived from the hawthorns
and the sea-anemones ; but this majestic stanzaic ode,
begirt with strophe and antistrophe, is too cumbrous for
its subject, and the attention wanders long before we
reach the inevitable and so expected passage about
Victor Hugo. A similar sense of tedium assails the
reader of " On the Cliffs ", a sense almost of irritation
that so much fine writing should have been expended
on Sappho, a fine poet, it may be supposed, but not one
who can so seriously be apprehended from the tattered
fragments that remain. Here again, in this insensate
Sappho-worship, we have an instance of Swinburne's
subjection to his own schoolboy impressions. It is
probable that some Sapphic fragment assumed for him
a purely adventitious importance when at Eton, and
from that small seed grew the quite disproportionate
forest of enthusiasm which choked the growth of other
and more important influences :

> Sappho—because I have known thee and loved, hast thou
> None other answer now ?
> As brother and sister were we, child and bird,
> Since thy first Lesbian word
> Flamed on me, and I knew not whence I knew
> This was the song that struck my whole soul through,
> Pierced my keen spirit of sense with edge more keen,
> Even when I knew not,—even ere sooth was seen,—
> When thou wast but the tawny sweet winged thing
> Whose cry was but of spring.

Another instance of this exaggerated hero-worship

is furnished by the immense Birthday Ode to Victor Hugo, which consists of thirteen strophes, thirteen antistrophes, and thirteen epodes. In " On the Cliffs " Swinburne in the enthusiasm of the moment had inserted translations of certain of the Sapphic fragments; in the Birthday Ode he went a step further, and furnished a complete rhymed bibliography of the works of Victor Hugo. This detestable practice seemed to have struck Watts as very scholarly and original : we meet it frequently in subsequent doxologies. It is a safe rule to skip all such passages : one can see where they are coming from the explanatory notes which cluster in their wake.

There is one poem, however, in *Songs of the Springtides* of outstanding interest, of very remarkable illumination. It is entitled " Thalassius ", and is evidently intended to be autobiographical, even apologetic, in character. It is the story of a child abandoned on some desolate shore, though born of a union between Apollo and Cymothoe, the sun-god and the sea. This child is found and nurtured by a legendary figure, a composite idealisation of Landor, Hugo, and Mazzini : by him the boy is taught the love of love, the passion for liberty, the hatred of oppression, the hope of what is to come, the fear of worthlessness. Thus armed the boy sets " foot upon the spring-flowered ways " and meets with Love, whose mouth " was as the very rose of all men's youth ", who seemed at first a " dumb thing mild and hurtless ", who

> strayed with faint bare lily-lovely feet
> Helpless and flowerlike sweet.

Suddenly in the blind eyes of Love there burns " hard light and heat of laughter " ; his stature embraces the firmament; in a voice "that stilled the winds" Love cries and vanishes :

> O fool, my name is sorrow,
> Thou fool, my name is death.

Thereafter, in a fine corybantic passage, come the Maenads and the Bassarides ; satiety follows, and with satiety the thought of the sea, the instinct for ablution. The purification is accomplished ; the sea gives back to him the white wings of his childhood ; and at the close Apollo appears and utters the final benediction :

> Because thou hast loved nought mortal more than me,
> Thy father, and thy mother-hearted sea ;
> Because thou hast set thine heart to sing, and sold
> Life and life's love for song, God's living gold ;
> Because thou hast given thy flower and fire of youth
> To feed men's hearts with visions, truer than truth ;
> Because thou hast kept in those world-wandering eyes
> The light that makes me music of the skies ;
> Because thou hast heard with world-unwearied ears
> The music that puts light into the spheres ;
> Have therefore in thine heart and in thy mouth
> The sound of song that mingles north and south,
> The song of all the winds that sing of me,
> And in thy soul the sense of all the sea.

Can such a passage, can such a poem, be dismissed as merely rhetorical ? Swinburne was the least self-conscious of men, the least self-analytical. That he should have chosen for his apologia so penetrating an analogy argues a personal conviction deeper than many have supposed, and indicates a startling perception of his own isolation, of his own surpassing strangeness. It may seem merely fantastic for any man thus to represent himself as anadyomenos, as a sexless, ageless, earthless emanation of sun and sea ; as something potential rather than potent ; as something impervious to human rules of growth and development ; as " a manchild with an ungrown God's desire ". There are some of us, however, who will find " Thalassius " absolutely convincing, and who will regard it as constituting a very illuminating and intensive disclosure of the central core of Swinburne's temperament.

Already in *Studies in Song*, the second collection of poems which Swinburne published in 1880, the influence of Watts becomes apparent. We now enter upon " Mr. Swinburne's later development as a nature lover and poet of the sea ". " For the last thirty years ", wrote Watts in 1910, " his thoughts had been mainly absorbed in two subjects. The first of these was the study and contemplation of nature in various localities. The second . . . was childhood." The point that Watts overlooked was that Swinburne's genius did not lie in the direction of nature-poetry : he was too dynamic to acquire the necessary mood of static contemplation ; he was too unobservant, too insensitive, either to illumine or to interpret. He can make a fine use of similes, metaphors, or images drawn from natural objects, but when he approaches Nature directly the disabilities of his temperament become sadly apparent ; his nature poems are diffuse, ecstatic, and marred by repetition. Even in his treatment of the sea he breaks down completely when he ceases to be allusive and becomes descriptive : so long as the sea remained for him a lustral symbol of ablution and freedom he could write magnificently and as if a beam of sunshine flying along the waves ; but when Watts set him down upon the parade at Cromer he could produce only a jumble of stock epithets—some portentous dithyramb on the lines of " By the North

Sea ". And one exclaims despairingly, " What ails us
with thee, who art wind and air ? "

For this reason I would not advise people to read
with undue expectancy *Studies in Song*. They will find
among them an ode to Landor followed by a string of
footnotes to explain the bibliography. They will find
an ode to Mazzini, some lines to Orsini, an excellent
translation from Aristophanes, and three long sea
pieces, competent but wholly uninspired. A similar
warning must be uttered against the *Century of
Roundels* of 1883 and the *Midsummer Holiday* of 1884.
The later volume is wholly uninteresting, the former
interesting only as a reflection of his early moods at
Putney, and as an illustration of the deplorable poetry
which, in spite of Hugo's *L'Art d'être grand-père*, is
generally written about children. The *Century of
Roundels*, or, more properly, *Rondeaux*, was, as Sir
Edmund Gosse informs us, written by Swinburne for
the purpose of self-discipline and in the realisation that
his flowing Pindaric facility was getting somewhat out
of hand. Those of them that do not deal with the
charms of infants are pleasant enough, and there is
real interest in the mood of gentle remorse which
inspired such pieces as " In Harbour ", " Had I
Wist ", and " Recollections ". Nor can I omit to
mention and to praise the exquisite skill and concision of " A Flowerpiece by Fantin ". But the
several verses addressed to Watts's nephew, little
Bertie Mason, seldom rise above the level of the
following :

> A baby shines as bright
> If winter or if May be
> On eyes that keep in sight
>   A baby.

> Though dark the skies or grey be,
> It fills our eyes with light
> If midnight or midday be.
>
> Love hails it, day and night,
> The sweetest thing that may be,
> Yet cannot praise aright
>   A baby.

We turn with relief from nonsense such as this to the *Heptalogia* of 1880, in which Swinburne collected and published anonymously seven parodies, composed at different periods since 1859, upon Patmore, Tennyson, the two Brownings, and Lord Lytton. The skit on Mrs. Browning is particularly ingenious, while the collection is further enhanced by a convincing parody of his own anapaestic and alliterative method :

> From the depth of the dreamy decline of the dawn through a
>   notable nimbus of nebulous noonshine,
> Pallid and pink as the palm of the flag-flower that flickers with
>   fear of the flies as they float.

The chill reception accorded to *Songs of the Spring-tides*, *Studies in Song*, *A Century of Roundels*, and *A Midsummer Holiday* appears for a while to have discouraged Swinburne from further lyrical composition. The period from 1884 to 1889 was devoted to critical and dramatic work, notably to *Marino Faliero* and *Locrine*. In 1889, however, he again published a volume of poetry entitled *Poems and Ballads : Third Series*. Prominent among the poems of this compilation figures the " Commonweal ", in which the regicide of Balliol days celebrates the jubilee of " a blameless queen ", masking his inconsistency in studied platitudes, identifying Queen Victoria at first with England and, by this transition, with the sea.

" Pan and Thalassius " is also of interest, not merely

as being the final repudiation of the earth for the sea,
but because of the infinitely skilful and original metre
in which it is composed. The poem entitled " The
Interpreters " is noteworthy as indicating that there
were moments, even in his forty-ninth year, when
Swinburne felt that literature was after all subordinate
to life :

> Days dawn on us that make amends for many
> > Sometimes,
> When heaven and earth seem sweeter than any
> > Man's rhymes.
>
> Light had not all been quenched in France, or quelled
> > In Greece,
> Had Homer sung not, or had Hugo held
> > His peace.
>
> Had Sappho's self not left her word thus long
> > For token,
> 'The sea round Lesbos yet in waves of song
> > Had spoken.

Finally, the third series of *Poems and Ballads* is
memorable for the inclusion of some of the Border
ballads composed in 1864, while the rich wine of Pre-
Raphaelitism was coursing in his veins. Nor can I
refrain from quoting from that plaintive little elegy
called " To a Seamew ", in which the wistfulness of
his later life whispers for a moment behind the back of
Walter Watts :

> When I had wings, my brother,
> > Such wings were mine as thine :
> Such life my heart remembers
> In all as wild Septembers
> As this when life seems other,
> > Though sweet, than once was mine ;
> When I had wings, my brother,
> > Such wings were mine as thine.

.   .   .   .   .

> We are fallen, even we, whose passion
>   On earth is nearest thine ;
> Who sing, and cease from flying ;
> Who live, and dream of dying :
> Grey time, in time's grey fashion,
>   Bids wingless creatures pine :
> We are fallen, even we, whose passion
>   On earth is nearest thine.
>
> .   .   .   .   .
>
> Ah, well were I for ever,
>   Wouldst thou change lives with me,
> And take my song's wild honey,
> And give me back thy sunny
> Wide eyes that weary never,
>   And wings that search the sea ;
> Ah, well were I for ever,
>   Wouldst thou change lives with me.

For of all Swinburne's later poetry this poem almost alone fills me with a conviction of actual experience.

There are three further volumes of poetry which must be mentioned in this catalogue. There is *Astrophel* of 1894, which is redeemed from absolute dullness by the fine dedication to William Morris, by the " Ode to Eton ", by the elegies on Burton, Browning, and Bell Scott, and by the two poems to Tennyson. It will be noted that these poems are all connected with his pre-redemption life : the Putney poems, on the other hand, are but poor stuff indeed. There are some distressing verses on Ireland in which Watts's politics grimace behind a faded mask of *Songs before Sunrise*, and there is throughout a ghastly vulgarisation of his former style, of which the following lines are hardly an unfair illustration :

> In the grime and the gloom of November,
>   The bliss and the bloom of July
> Bade autumn rejoice and remember
>   The balm of the blossoms gone by.

> Would you know what moss-rose now it may be
>   That puts all the rest to the blush ?
> The flower was the face of a baby,
>   The moss was a bonnet of plush.

Equally regrettable are the majority of the poems which he published in his sixty-eighth year under the title of *A Channel Passage*.   By those who care for Swinburne's reputation this volume should be approached with great caution.   The danger of these poems is that they may create a sensation of repletion, and cast a momentary doubt on the sincerity and the integrity even of *Songs before Sunrise*.

Between *Astrophel* and *A Channel Passage* Swinburne composed a long narrative poem of really outstanding merit, in which his home-sickness for Northumberland pierces through the mists of Putney, and in which his own childhood lives again for him in the sunlight of gay adventure.   There is a rollicking note about *The Tale of Balen*, a light continuous movement as of an April brook hastening to the sea :

> And down a dim deep woodland way
> They rode between the boughs asway
> With flickering winds whose flash and play
> Made sunlight sunnier where the day
>   Laughed, leapt, and fluttered like a bird
> Caught in a light loose leafy net
> That earth for amorous heaven had set
> To hold and see the sundawn yet
>   And hear what morning heard.

The Tale of Balen comes as a breath of fresh Northumbrian air through the heavy plush curtains by which his later life was muffled : it is a welcome antidote to the weariness and lethargy induced by the poetry of his second period.

It remains to discuss the six plays that Swinburne

wrote during his sojourn at The Pines. In *Mary Stuart*, which was published in 1881, he completed his trilogy on the life and adventures of Mary, Queen of Scots. Although less diffuse than *Bothwell*, the play suffers equally from a centrifugal tendency, from an absence of dramatic synthesis. Obviously Swinburne's intention was, as in *Bothwell*, to picture Nemesis using the wrath and love of Mary Beaton as an instrument for revenging the betrayal of Chastelard. But here again he becomes involved in his own erudition, and loses himself in the hopeless confusion and obscurity of the Babington conspiracy and in the historical records of the Queen's trial. It is only in the second scene of Act IV., when the *motif* of *Chastelard* is at last allowed to predominate, that we catch for a fleeting moment the lyrical beauty of his earlier plays, and that the dramatic intention of the trilogy becomes again apparent. Nor can it be said that either *Bothwell* or *Mary Stuart* justifies the bright promise of *Chastelard*, or is worthy of the charming " Adieux à Marie Stuart " in which Swinburne with a delicately remorseful cadence took leave of this life-long obsession.

Marino Faliero represents a curious attempt to dramatise the inspiration of *Songs before Sunrise*, and to show how superficially both Byron and Delavigne had dealt with this somewhat inscrutable incident. For the Doge in Swinburne's play, although he begins by manifesting the petulant obstinacy of the tradition, ends by sweeping the whole action into one continuous apocalyptic monologue of his own, emerging as some prophetic and biblical figure prophesying the advent of Mazzini. A similar reversion to former inspiration is manifested in *Locrine*, a play which, in form at least, is even more lyrical than *Rosamund*, and which is of interest mainly as being an experiment, and not a very successful experiment, in the use of the rhymed couplet, and even of the sonnet, as a vehicle for dramatic dialogue. From *The Sisters* of 1892 I have already quoted, as also from the beautiful dedication to Lady Mary Gordon. The interest of the play is mainly autobiographical, but one can admire the audacity with which Swinburne endeavours to introduce the blood and thunder of the Elizabethan formula into the drawing-room at Bonchurch. The two final plays of *Rosamund, Queen of the Lombards*, and *The Duke of Gandia*, each represent a gallant attempt to achieve dramatic concentration, but they are both what have been called " study-plays ", and such interest as they evoke is neither very deep nor very continuous. For if the drama of action is in fact a modern possibility, it requires a greater knowledge of life, a keener insight into character, and a more vital grasp of reality than was possessed, even before the Putney period, by the unterrestrial Swinburne.

I have kept for my conclusion the discussion of *Tristram of Lyonesse*, the work which Swinburne intended to be his masterpiece, and which is certainly the most important of all the poems that he composed or completed after 1879. The ambition to write an epic round the Tristram legend had germinated at Eton, and it is clear that several false starts were made even before the first published fragments of 1858. In 1871 he again tackled the subject, and he then wrote, almost at a sitting, the magnificent invocation to Love which still figures as the prelude to the poem. Again and again during the years that followed he would return

N

to this epic, and compose more " parcels of Tristram ",
but it was not till the summer of 1881 that he set himself
seriously to the task of its completion. The poem was
finished in April 1882, and published in the following
July, a month after the first performance in London of
Wagner's *Tristan*. The effect of its appearance was
somewhat marred by the insertion in the same volume
of many dull and unnecessary verses, or, as Swinburne
called them, " Songs of Innocence ". It was Watts
who had insisted upon this padding, hoping thereby to
soften and to mitigate what he considered to be the
luscious and indeed amorous tone of the main poem.

The high level set by the prelude, with its jewelled
enumeration of the Zodiac of famous lovers, is not of
course maintained throughout the nine episodes which
follow. Nor did Swinburne ever attempt to execute
his original intention of giving to the poem either an
epic or a continuously narrative form. His purpose,
as he himself explained, was merely to present " a
succession of dramatic scenes and pictures with
descriptive settings of backgrounds ", but the result is
essentially a lyrical poem cast in an episodic narrative
form. Not that the dramatic element is nugatory :
the death of Tristram is recounted with fine dramatic
instinct, and the early episode of the love potion, the
cause of the whole tragedy, is rendered with vigorous
intensity :

> And all their life changed in them, for they quaffed
> Death ; if it be death so to drink, and fare
> As men who change and are what these twain were.
> And shuddering with eyes full of fear and fire,
> And heart-stung with a serpentine desire,
> He turned and saw the terror in her eyes
> That yearned upon him shining in such wise
> As a star midway in the midnight fixed.

Their Galahault was the cup, and she that mixed ;
Nor other hand there needed, nor sweet speech
To lure their lips together ; each on each
Hung with strange eyes and hovered as a bird
Wounded, and each mouth trembled for a word ;
Their heads neared, and their hands were drawn in one,
And they saw dark, though still the unsunken sun
Far through fine rain shot fire into the south ;
And their four lips became one burning mouth.

Inevitably there are a few passages in which Swinburne's fluency, in which his exaggerated consideration
for his authorities, lead him into diffuseness, but these
passages are comparatively rare, and as a whole the
poem moves gently in a Celtic twilight and to the
tremulous cadence inspired by

The music of the silence of the place,
The confluence and the refluence of the sea.

Throughout the poem the sea is thus treated symbolically and as an undertone to the development, and it
is in the " light and sound and darkness of the sea "
that it majestically concludes.

Tristram of Lyonesse is, even as it stands, so noble
an achievement that one is left wondering how it is
that it just fails to be a masterpiece, why it is that the
high promise of the Prelude is not maintained. Sir
Edmund Gosse is inclined to attribute its comparative
failure to Swinburne's " total want of energy in the
narrative ". I fear that it is not only about the
narrative that there hangs a sense of lethargy : one
derives an impression that the poem had lain far too
long on his hands, and that, in spite of its exquisite
finish, the zest had left him when he came to gather
its disjointed fragments into a whole. It is sad to
reflect that, had he not at that time been diverted into
the dusty corridors of *Bothwell*, he might well have

completed the poem between 1871 and 1874, and have given to it an even greater force and elevation, nor have left us questioning :

Yea, but what then ?   Albeit all this were thus,
And soul smote soul and left it ruinous,
And love led love as eyeless men lead men,
Through chance by chance to deathward—Ah, what then ?

CHAPTER X

No study of Swinburne as an English man of letters would be complete without a survey of his work as scholar and critic, if only because the lifelong assiduity with which he worked in the mines of Elizabethan drama, the lifelong zest with which he celebrated those literary heroes whose works had penetrated to his inner consciousness, constitutes, as it were, the keel of his heavily canvassed vessel, giving to it a solidity, a poise, and even a direction, which it might otherwise have lacked. His interesting contributions to the *Spectator* in the early 'sixties are not easily available, but the majority of his subsequent articles for the *Fortnightly* were collected and issued either posthumously or during his lifetime, and reach, together with his published monographs, the respectable total of twelve stout volumes :

1868. William Blake.
1875. Essays and Studies.
1875. George Chapman.
1877. A Note on Charlotte Brontë.
1880. A Study of Shakespeare.
1886. A Study of Victor Hugo.
1886. Miscellanies.
1894. Studies in Prose and Poetry.
1908. The Age of Shakespeare.

1909. Shakespeare.
1913. Charles Dickens.
1918. The Age of Shakespeare (Vol. II.).

From 1905 also dates the publication of his novel *Love's Cross-currents*, which had been written in 1876, and which is interesting both for autobiographical reasons and because it contains a curiously un-Swinburnian element of the mundane, the analytical, almost of the cynical. His other novel, *Lesbia Brandon*, is also, I understand, about to see the light of day; and it is to be feared that the old misconception of Swinburne will thereby, in many simple hearts, be wholly gratuitously revived.

It is not, however, on his novels, and still less on his letters, that any estimate of Swinburne as a writer of English prose can be based: his work as a critic, whether of general literature or within the highly specialised radius of the Elizabethan drama, is of sufficient weight and scholarship to give him a definite and independent place in the history of English criticism. "He put new life", says Professor Mackail, "into poetical criticism, gave it a new range and scope and brilliance, in something of the same way as he discovered or revealed new potentialities in poetry itself."

What, therefore, are the especial qualities of Swinburne as a critic? In the forefront, perhaps, we should place assiduity—an almost superhuman industry which enabled him, for instance, to plough through the unexplored thickets of Blake's prophetic books, or to analyse and to interpret the most forbidding and the most obscure of Elizabethan dramatists. And in the second place we must place judgement.

Not merely the refined taste which could recognise the
merits of Crabbe and Collins, or could prefer the prose
of Musset to his " fitful and febrile " poetry. Not
even the perspicacity which could place Stendhal above
the then still popular Merimée or could point out to an
obtuse public the merits of Whistler or of Meredith.
Not merely a felicity of analysis which could thus
portray Dryden : " He had nothing in him of plebeian
fire, and nothing of patrician chivalry. He had, as we
may not doubt, a just and due sense of honesty, but
scarcely . . . a high or tender sense of honour." Nor
is the essential value of Swinburne's critical work to be
looked for only in that moral daring which could proclaim that Browning was not obscure, and Tennyson
scarcely lucid ; it is to be found in a particular
quality of illumination, in a gift of judgement which,
in his serener moments (and they were more frequent
than might be supposed), amounted almost to vision,
and through which he anticipated, if he did not create,
a more enlightened opinion on such poets as Coleridge,
Byron, Tennyson, Arnold, Morris, and Rossetti—an
opinion which we, with our advantage of increased
perspective, may perhaps regard as obvious, but which
was then unquestionably original and daring.

These merits of assiduity, of zest, and of vision have
been very generally recognised as constituting Swinburne's major claim to importance as a critic. I feel,
however, that we are apt to overlook, or at least to
underestimate, the very vitalising influence which his
critical studies exercised upon the generation which
developed between 1862 and 1877. As M. Reul has
pointed out, he stood for his age in a position midway
between the doctrinaire criticism of Matthew Arnold

and the aesthetic criticism of Walter Pater. His endeavour admittedly was to expound the work before him, not to trace the principles upon which that work might or might not have been based. His method was the method of sympathy, of generosity, of enthusiasm ; he sought always for what was best, feeling that an author should be judged solely by his masterpieces and not by his defects. " For love ", he wrote, " and judgement must be one in those who would look into such high and lovely things."

It was not, however, Swinburne's burning zest and admiration which alone led the young men of the 'sixties to read the *Fortnightly* articles with an ever-kindled excitement. Although his critical work was in a sense empirical, yet it never became merely incidental or opportunist. For Swinburne grappled continuously, courageously, and, above all, intelligently, with the problem of Art *v.* Morals, a problem which, in the age of the *Idylls*, was one of burning topical interest. As was inevitable, he spoke for the emancipation of art from all extraneous tyrannies, he preached the doctrine of poetry for poetry's sake. " Art ", he wrote, " for art's sake first of all, and afterwards we may suppose all the rest shall be added to her (or if not she need hardly be overmuch concerned), but from the man who falls to artistic work with a moral purpose shall be taken away even that which he has—whatever of capacity for doing well in either way he may have at starting." These words, be it remembered, were published in 1868. In 1872 he expanded the doctrine further, protecting the dignity of poetry from the misconception which such a theory might instil into the unwary.

Swinburne was too great a man of letters to
appreciate or forgive the dilettante ; and the qualifica-
tions which he imposed upon poetic licence are as
rigid and as virile as those of Carducci himself.
" The well-known formula ", he wrote, " of art for
art's sake . . . has like other doctrines a true side to
it and an untrue. Taken as an affirmative, it is a
precious and everlasting truth. No work of art has
any worth or life in it that is not done on the absolute
terms of art. . . . On the other hand we refuse to
admit that art of the highest kind may not ally itself
with moral or religious passion, with the ethics or the
politics of a nation or an age. . . . In a word, the
doctrine of art for art is true in the positive sense, false
in the negative ; sound as an affirmative, unsound as a
prohibition."

While, therefore, defining and qualifying this conception of the function of poetry, Swinburne lays down
for the poet an exacting standard of sincerity and of
ideal. The poet must follow his star with unswerving
fidelity ; he must throw into his work his own idealisation of his own capacities ; he must possess " an ardent
harmony ", a " heat of spiritual life " ; his imagination
must be dominant, liberated, convincing, muscular ;
" there must be an instinct and a resolution of excellence
which will allow no shortcoming or malformation of
thought or word " ; the work must be " serious,
simple, perfect ". Only by such self-discipline, by the
fires of such sincerity, can the poet aspire to the
" sublime ", in the sense that such auroral poets as
Villon and Marlowe attained sublimity. And in the
end : " The full cause of the full effect achieved by
poetry of the first order can be defined and expounded

with exact precision and certitude of accuracy by no strength of argument or sublety of definition. . . . The test of the highest poetry is that it eludes all tests."

Such was the stern and virile purpose which inspired the critical attitude of Swinburne, and which, when realised, enables us to see in his own poetical work a greater seriousness, a more muscular control, than might be apprehended merely from abandoning ourselves to the smooth flux of his amazing fluency. His works on Shakespeare and the Elizabethan dramatists, being predominantly interpretative, erudite, and expository, stand in a somewhat separate category. His deep knowledge of the period, his lifelong research and industry, his amazing memory, rendered him a distinguished Shakespearian scholar, a dominant specialist in his subject. The frequent monographs, the more frequent articles, the protracted controversy even with Furnivall, became after 1879 the real " action " of his existence, to which the daily life at The Pines was but a neutral, scarcely apprehended, background. Further and further, as the years proceeded, did he retreat into his folios, losing finally all touch with the present, accepting it vaguely and at second hand from Watts, uncertain finally whether *Arden of Feversham* was more, or less, contemporaneous than 1895. This intensive process renders his Elizabethan studies a little disconcerting to the general reader, for of the general reader Swinburne had no conception whatsoever, finding it difficult to imagine that every adult man and woman had not attained to exactly the same level of Shakespearian scholarship as he had reached himself. It is not merely that his works

on the Elizabethan drama abound in allusion, are based
on an assumption of knowledge, which strikes no chord
even of reminiscence in the brain of average man, but
also that the uniformity of Swinburne's praise and
admiration makes confusion worse confounded, since
he does but plant rambler roses in place of the brambles
which he clears away. Thus when we read that Cyril
Tourneur is but a lesser Shakespeare, or that Webster
is the equal of Aeschylus, we may well feel ashamed at
our own dulled perceptions ; but when the same
uncontrolled hyperbole is poured out on lesser melo-
dramatists, the gorge rises and we feel not unwilling to
join M. Jusserand in his pilgrimage to Saint-Étienne-
du-Mont.

Although, however, Swinburne's critical work upon
the Elizabethan and Jacobean dramatists is no very
useful guide for the uninitiated, and although we
may find in such slim works as Rupert Brooke's
Cambridge essay a more convenient handbook, yet it
must be realised that our impatience with these monographs is due largely to the fact that the average interest
in the subject concentrates upon the relation between
these lesser dramatists and Shakespeare, a relation
which Swinburne's non-comparative method tends only
to obscure. Taken by themselves and on the ground
that they were composed by a scholar for specialists,
these essays and monographs, particularly those which
date from the earlier period, are admirably conceived.
The early essay on Chapman, in spite of the turgid
exaggeration which it absorbs from the subject, did
much to place that exuberant author in the high position
that he now occupies ; the study of John Ford is ex-
cellently balanced, and contains a welcome comparative

analysis in which Swinburne discusses with unusual
stringency and concision the respective manners of
Ford, Massinger, Tourneur, Middleton, Decker, and
Chapman ; the examination of Ben Jonson, in spite of
its rhetorical excess, and the misplaced digression on
the *Discoveries*, commands respect, and contains some
stimulating classification ; while the shorter essay on
Beaumont and Fletcher, those " great if not blameless
dramatists ", is a scholarly and lucid endeavour to
appraise and demarcate the respective merits and
composition of the " Dioscuri of English Poetry ".
Of Shakespeare himself Swinburne has much to say
which is illuminating rather than original ; his treatment of the plays is so eclectic as to become almost
episodic ; his concentration upon the poetical rather
than on the dramatic element is interesting, and gives a
consistency to his exposition which it would otherwise
lack ; while his early investigations into the development of metrical form in Shakespeare enables him to
throw a useful light on the vexed question of collabora-
tion and on the dates of such plays as *Henry VIII.*,
of *Richard II.*, and of *Richard III.* It was his revolu-
tionary views on these latter points which initiated the
fierce controversy with the Shakspeare Society.

Although, therefore, Swinburne's literary criticism
displays the qualities of scholarship, industry, and
vision, and although his treatment of the theory of
art for art's sake produced a profound and wholesome
effect upon his contemporaries, yet it must be admitted
that those temperamental defects which we have noted
in discussing his poetry exercised upon his prose an
influence even more deleterious and persistent. His
lack of constructional power, his inability to conceive

of what he wished to say until he began to say it, his endless digressions and improvisations, combine to create an impression of diffuseness and redundancy which, as in his poetry, mars the secret of the whole. His literary judgements, when isolated, appear brilliant and convincing; but in their actual context they glimmer but vaguely to a reader already wearied and confused by the dust-storms through which he has passed. That curious sense of mirage which flickers so persistently above the work of Swinburne is increased in his critical studies by his constant and hysterical exaggerations, by his persistent refusal to consider any shade or gradation between the dazzling white of sublimity and the coal blackness of those writers for whom he does not happen to care. Sympathy is admittedly essential to criticism, and the praise of famous men can provide at fit moments an enlightening stimulus; but sympathy should be mated with discrimination, and praise should keep careful accounts—should be conscious that the English language is not over rich in terms of approval. The reckless lavishness of Swinburne's generosity, the extent to which he is both penny-foolish and pound-foolish in his largesse, is constantly landing him in awkward situations; for having already expended all his superlatives in the rambling course of his argument, he often reaches the portals of his main thesis with not a " divine ", not even a " magnificent " or a " superb ", left in his pocket, and has to turn away with some such face-saving phrase as " The passionate glory of its rapid and profound music fills the sense with too deep and sharp a delight to leave breathing-space for any thought of analytic or apologetic work ". A further element of disturbance is the constant intrusion into his criticism of a shrill note of the biassed and the personal. Again and again the reader becomes suddenly conscious that a hectic flush is spreading over the page ; and he looks up to find beside him, not the wise and gentle scholar whom he had taken as his guide, but a raging schoolboy, who proceeds forthwith to shriek falsetto insults in his ear. In the early studies these outbursts are comparatively few, comparatively restrained ; but in the later criticisms they multiply exceedingly, and leave behind them a distressing sense of irresponsibility, which robs his judgements of the very real value and conviction they should possess and inspire. These outbursts of violence might well be ignored could they readily be isolated from the main tenor of his argument. But such isolation is not always possible. In the first place he loses his temper so suddenly, so unexpectedly, that the reader is caught napping. I will quote but one passage to illustrate my meaning. Swinburne is writing about Keats :

The " Ode to a Nightingale ", one of the finest master-pieces of human work in all time and for all ages, is immediately preceded in all editions now current by some of the most vulgar and fulsome doggerel ever whimpered by a vapid and effeminate rhymester in the sickly stage of whelphood.

Now Swinburne's real intention was to protest against the bad taste of editors in including too many juvenilia in collected editions, but at the thought of these editors, at the realisation of how much he himself would mind if the " Triumph of Gloriana " were to appear prefixed to *Songs before Sunrise*, the blood seethes to his brain, and he brings his stick down smash, not on the head of the absent editor, but on the head of the unoffending

Keats, who simply happened, all careless, to be there.
There are moments even when these jets of childish
temper, issuing in a splutter of alliterative invective,
lead the kindly Swinburne into sudden and almost
unintentional phrases of real cruelty, such as his brutal
and gratuitous lunge at John Addington Symonds.
But this particular form of outburst is fortunately rare.

A second circumstance which renders it difficult to
isolate Swinburne's bias from his critical judgement
is that the latter is throughout permeated by those
idolatries and hatreds which became an organic portion
of all his concepts. His hero-worship was something
deeper and more pathological than what he himself
called " a pure excess of admiration for things indeed
admirable, of delight in things indeed delightful ". It
affected his life and his poetry : profoundly it affected
his literary opinions. It was inevitable, of course, that a
large proportion of his critical work, as of his poetry,
should have been devoted to the praise of Victor Hugo,
nor are we surprised to hear that writer described as
" the greatest European poet since the days of Dante "
or as " the greatest dramatist that the world has seen
since the death of Shakespeare ". But when we find
Swinburne speaking seriously of Hugo's " burning
sincerity ", comparing him seriously to Blake, speaking
in all fervour of the " auroral resonance and radiance of
the luminous *Orientales* ", we come to realise that in
the presence of his deity he passed into some ecstatic
trance, becoming incapable thereafter of all but auto-
matic gestures of adoration, of mystic incantations
muttered to the rhythmic beating of a gong. This
were, indeed, a pardonable aberration, a flash merely of
the inspired loyalty which lay at the root of his nature,

did it not extend to and colour his views on other writers and on other subjects. It is not always very easy to disentangle the intricate subconscious ramifications of Swinburne's Hugo-complex. It is simple enough to attribute to this obsession his dislike of Sainte - Beuve or his appreciation of Cladel; but the process becomes more complicated when we realise that he flames into enthusiasm for Tennyson's " Rizpah " (a commendable poem, doubtless, but not a very satisfying cause for hysterics), because Victor Hugo had been oppressed by Napoleon III., and Napoleon III. had been acquiesced in by De Musset, and De Musset had recently, in the last volume of Taine, been placed higher than Tennyson. Throughout Swinburne's critical work we find traces of the indirect influence of similar obsessions, of which that for Hugo was only the most predominant. His attack on Byron was inspired partly by his love of Landor, partly by his love of Shelley, and to the same cause we owe much, but not the whole, of his evident distaste for Matthew Arnold. His unreasoning, persistent, and curiously venomous hatred of Carlyle was not unconnected with his affection for Lamb; whereas his admiration of Coleridge rendered Hazlitt anathema. " We don't mention Hazlitt's name here," hurriedly whispered Watts-Dunton to a visitor who, having unwittingly broached that subject, had paused in dismay at Swinburne's sudden expression of " frozen anger ".

Such prejudices and preventions may well be disconcerting, but they are at least consistent. Throughout his fifty years of critical work Swinburne was guilty of only three apostasies : he repudiated Whistler, he repudiated Baudelaire, he repudiated Walt Whitman ; and in each case he was acting not as a free agent, but under the dictation of Watts-Dunton.

A further and more serious bar to the full appreciation of Swinburne's critical writings is the appalling prose in which they are often written. His violent rhodomontades, each word flanked by double alliterative adjectives, his incessant superlatives, his unending sentences rising in a reiterative crescendo, his false analogies and incoherent similes, are jumbled together in a fervid rush of encumbered verbiage. It is not a cascade which we witness ; it is something more than a torrent ; it is as if a congested river were to flood fiercely through the streets of some populated city, bearing on its churning waters the riches and the ordures, the damask and the dusters of the town. In contrast to the high technical level always maintained by his poetry, Swinburne's worst prose is incomparably different from his best. And let it be remembered that his best prose is very good indeed. It seems, indeed, almost incredible from the point of view of style alone that the man who could have written *Whitmania* could also have written the magnificent conclusion to Blake, or a final sentence of such perfection as : " A more noble memory is hardly left us ; and it is not for his sake that we should contend to do him honour ". Even more astonishing are the sudden lapses in the same paragraph, from the language of Dryden to a language which can only be called Swinburne's own. The following passage is an example of these sudden stylistic skids :

But it is useless to insist on such simple and palpable truths ; for ignorance will never understand that knowledge is attainable, and impotence will never admit that ability may be competent. " Do you suppose it as easy to write a song as to write an epic ? " said Béranger to Lucien Bonaparte. Nor would it be as easy for a most magnanimous mouse of a Calibanic poeticule to write a ballad, a roundel, or a virelai, after the noble fashion of Chaucer, as to gabble at any length like a thing most brutish in the blank and blatant jargon of epic or idyllic stultiloquence.

It happens that the manuscript of the essay from which this outburst is chosen is now in the possession of Balliol College. It is clear from this manuscript that the last six lines quoted were inserted by Swinburne subsequently and in a burst of hot temper on re-reading what he had written ; it is curious also to observe how the crescendo of his anger is reflected in his childish handwriting as it would indubitably have been had he read the passage aloud ; for the words are written larger and larger as his excitement waxes, and the final " stultiloquence " is black and enormous, signifying a shriek of defiance.

These strange lapses from his own standard of stylistic behaviour are not indeed the only flaws which impede the purity and disturb the intellectual reception of Swinburne's criticism. His humour, which rarely attains a high level of subtlety, is often of the variety which Sir A. Quiller-Couch has called "polysyllabic", and he very frequently indulges in jocose euphemia :

Another great name here somewhat woefully misrepresented is that of Thackeray : whose *White Squall* is now and then rather too provocative of such emotions as Nature's might provoke in the digestive economy of a bad sailor.

His irony, again, often misses its effect by becoming too stridently personal, or too portentously elaborate : the

fun which he pokes at Matthew Arnold is sly enough ;
but the elaborate comic business of " Tennyson or
Darwin ? " is infinitely depressing ; while his attempts
to imitate the manner of the old Scotch Reviewers are
pathetic in their inefficacy :

" Did you ask dulcet rhymes from me ? " inquires Mr.
Whitman of some extraordinary if not imaginary inter-
locutor; and proceeds with some not ineffective energy of
expression to explain that " I lull nobody—and you will
never understand me ", " No, my dear good sir—or
camerado, if that be the most courteous and conventional
address " (a modest reader might deferentially reply) : " not
in the wildest visions of a distempered slumber could I ever
have dreamed of doing anything of the kind. Nor do we
ask them ever from each other and inferior scribes or bards
as the humble Homer, the modest Milton, or the obsolete
and narrow-minded Shakespeare—poets of sickly feudality,
of hide-bound classicism, of effete and barbarous incom-
petence."

Passages such as this, faults of style and discretion
such as those that I have already indicated, occur with
frequency in all Swinburne's critical work, and with
particular frequency in the volumes which he published
after 1879. They must not blind us to the value of
that work, or even to its high technical proficiency and
attainment. Should any reader doubt Swinburne's
capacity for lucid exposition, let him read the essay on
Ford, or the *Notes on the Text of Shelley* ; should he
question his penetration, let him read the beautiful
analysis which figures on page 245 of *Blake*, the magnificently concise estimate of *King Lear*, or the essay on
Wordsworth and Byron ; should the critic's discrimination be doubted, then the essay on *Collins* can serve as
antidote ; and for the final test of his value as a writer
of English prose, let reference be made to the Pateresque

passage which figures on pages 317-319 of *Essays and Studies*, to the analysis of Rossetti's manner contained in *Some Pictures of 1868*, and above all to the last three pages of *Blake*. For it is no mean achievement for so voluminous a poet, for so intensive a scholar, to have produced at least two critical works of general interest, of enduring importance ; to have produced the *Study of Shakespeare*, which Professor Mackail has called "one of those works of illuminating and creative criticism which take rank as classics ", and to have produced *William Blake*, which in the words of Edward Thomas must remain " his one wholly necessary and perhaps unfading book of prose ".

The sketch of Swinburne's life and life-work has now been completed : there is no need to draw a picture of his fading years. The thing has been done by Sir Edmund Gosse, and it has been done by lesser hands. The most vivid portrait of the final phase is of course to be found in "No. 2 The Pines ". In this wide-read masterpiece Mr. Beerbohm has been able, as no one else, to write with humour but without jocose disparagement of Swinburne's suburban infirmary, and to achieve thereby a real sympathy and even liking for Watts-Dunton—an attitude of amused veneration which adds conviction to the vivid but delicate water-colour which he has drawn of the poet himself. No one better than Mr. Beerbohm has been able to capture and to convey the elusive charm of Swinburne, his air " at once noble and roguish, proud and skittish " ; his hands that " fluttered helplessly, touchingly, unceasingly " ; that something indefinable about him, that "something—boyish . . . ? girlish ? Childish, rather:

something of a beautifully well-bred child." For such, in essentials, is the impression which should remain.

In November of 1903, Swinburne, who prided himself on his indifference to the English climate, fell ill with pneumonia. At one moment his life was despaired of, and pessimistic bulletins appeared in the London press. He emerged from this illness with his lungs seriously affected, and the shrunken, hesitating appearance of the suddenly aged. The routine continued. It had become for him the only interpretation of external life : there were still the hawthorns and the perambulators on Wimbledon Common ; there was still the *Daily Telegraph* in the morning, and at tea-time the *Pall Mall Gazette* ; there was still the firelight flickering on the backs of his folios ; the gentle hissing of the acetylene gas. It was true that Watts-Dunton had been married in 1905. Or *was* it true ? Things had become so indistinct for him and muffled. So very indistinct. And then, on 31st March 1909, Watts-Dunton fell ill with influenza. This inevitably entailed some dislocation of their daily programme : the facts have been recorded by Mrs. Watts-Dunton :

Punctually at the appointed hour a tap was heard at the bedroom door, and there stood the Bard patiently awaiting permission to enter. He walked straight up to Walter's bedside and took a seat beside him. He had *Ivanhoe* in his hand all ready to begin. Before reading he gave a brief synopsis of the events occurring in the preceding chapter, and of those about to follow—a usual custom with him when reading a book they both knew well. Then, looking at me for an instant, expecting me either to get up and leave them alone, or sit where I was and listen, he turned to the place where they had left off the day before and asked, " Shall we begin ? " But Walter suggested that he might catch his cold if he sat next him for even half an hour, and suggested that they should postpone the reading till to-morrow, when they would be able to continue as usual. Swinburne looked woefully disappointed at being thus banished, and turning his gaze in my direction he enquired, " And will Clara stay and read it to you then ? " Walter assured him I would do nothing of the kind, and promised that only he should continue the narrative, explaining that as he was really not at all well, the doctor thought it advisable that I should be at hand to wait on him.

Swinburne appeared satisfied with this answer, and expressed his sorrow at his friend's condition. He seemed depressed, and just before leaving the room he said to me with rather a pathetic ring in his voice, and more than a suspicion of a sigh, " Ah, you are the privileged one ! " . . .

The next day, April 1, was wet and windy, but Swinburne went for his walk as usual and without a coat ; that evening he looked " weary and listless ", and on the following morning " Walter sent a very peremptory message to him absolutely forbidding him to go out ". Such a message was already unnecessary. By April 3 Swinburne had again developed the early symptoms of pneumonia; by April 5, his seventy-third birthday, he was too ill to open the telegrams that had arrived. The second lung was rapidly affected ; he suffered but little pain, and in his delirium he would gently murmur the choruses of Aeschylus and Sophocles. He died on the morning of April 10. He was buried at Bonchurch, a few yards only from the gardens of East Dene, a few yards only from the sea.

APPENDIX I

CHRONOLOGICAL TABLE

	Biography.	Main Publications.
	Born April 5, 1837.	
AGE.		
12.	Easter 1849. Goes to Eton.	
16.	July 1853. Leaves Eton.	
18.	July 1855. Visits Germany.	
18.	Jan. 1856. Goes to Balliol.	
20.	Apr. 1857. Friendship with Nichol.	1857. Article on Congreve in *Imperial Dictionary.*
20.	Nov. 1857. Meets Pre-Raphaelites.	
20.	Dec. 1857. " Undergraduate Papers."	Dec. 1857–Mar. 1858. Undergraduate Papers.
21.	June 1858. Fails for Newdigate. Friendship with Lady Trevelyan.	
22.	Nov. 1859—Oct. 1860. At Navestock.	
23.	Oct. 1860. Returns to Oxford.	1860. Queen Mother and Rosamond.
23.	Dec. 1860. Leaves Oxford. Visits Italy.	
23.	Jan. 1861. Settles in London.	
25.	? Feb. 1862. Refused by Miss Simon.	1862. Articles and poems in *Spectator.*
25.	Oct. 1862. Living with Rossetti.	
25.	Mar. 1863. In Paris.	1864. The Children of the Chapel. Dead Love.
26.	Mar. 1864. Visits Landor in Florence.	1865. Atalanta in Calydon (April). Chastelard.
27.	Oct. 1864. Leaves Rossetti.	
29.	May 1866. Lady Trevelyan dies.	1866. Laus Veneris. Poems and Ballads (July). Cleopatra. Notes on Poems and Reviews.

AGE	Biography.	Main Publications.
30. Apr. 1867.	Meets Mazzini.	1867. A Song of Italy.
		Articles in *Fortnightly* begin.
.. July ..	Composes Baudelaire ode.	
	Health failing.	
31. July 1868.	At Étretat with George Powell.	1868. Siena.
32. July 1869.	Nearly drowned at Étretat.	William Blake.
	At Vichy with Richard Burton.	
		1870. Ode on Proclamation of the French Republic.
33. Jan. 1871.	Meets Edmund Gosse.	1871. First Act of Bothwell.
34. Sept. 1871.	In Scotland with Jowett.	Songs before Sunrise.
35. Oct. 1872.	Quarrels with Howell.	
	Meets Walter Watts.	
36. Sept. 1873.	Watts becomes his man of business.	
		1874. Bothwell.
		1875. George Chapman.
		Songs of Two Nations.
		Essays and Studies.
38. July 1875.	Composes *Erechtheus* in Suffolk.	1876. Erechtheus.
38. Jan. 1876.	Controversy with Shakspeare Society.	
39. May 1876.	To Channel Islands with Nichol.	
39. Mar. 1877.	Death of Admiral Swinburne.	
40. Jan. 1878.	With Nichol at Glasgow.	1878. Poems and Ballads: Second Series.
41. July–Dec. 1878.	Health failing.	
42. Aug. 1879.	Complete collapse.	
42. Sept. 1879.	Taken to Putney.	
		1880. Songs of the Springtides.
		A Study of Shakespeare.
		Studies in Song.
		The Heptalogia.
		1881. Mary Stuart.

AGE.	Biography.		Main Publications.
45.	Nov. 1882.	Visits Hugo in Paris.	1882. Tristram of Lyonesse.
46.	July 1883.	At Cromer with Watts.	1883. A Century of Roundels.
47.	July 1884.	In Norfolk with Watts.	1884. A Midsummer Holiday.
			1885. Marino Faliero.
			1886. Miscellanies.
			A Study of Victor Hugo.
50.	July 1887.	At Lancing with Watts.	1887. The Jubilee.
			Locrine.
51.	Oct. 1888.	At Lancing again.	
			1889. A Study of Ben Jonson.
			Poems and Ballads : Third Series.
			1892. The Sisters.
			1894. Astrophel.
			Studies in Prose and Poetry.
59.	Nov. 1896.	Lady Jane Swinburne dies.	1896. The Tale of Balen.
			1899. A Channel Passage.
			Rosamund, Queen of the Lombards.
66.	Nov. 1903.	First attack of pneumonia.	1904. A Channel Passage, and other Poems.
			1905. Love's Cross-currents.
68.	Dec. 1905.	Walter Watts marries.	1908. The Duke of Gandia.
			The Age of Shakespeare.
73.	Apr. 10, 1909.	Dies of pneumonia.	

Posthumous.

1909. Three Plays of Shakespeare.
Shakespeare.
1913. Charles Dickens.
1917. Posthumous Poems.
1919. Contemporaries of Shakespeare.

APPENDIX II

A LIST OF USEFUL AUTHORITIES

[The more important are marked with an asterisk.]

Swinburne's Poems and Ballads : A Criticism. By W. M. Rossetti. J. C. Hotten, 1866.

The Fleshly School of Poetry. By Robert Buchanan. A pamphlet issued by Strahan & Co. in 1872.

A. C. Swinburne : A Study. By Theodore Wratislaw. Greening & Co., 1900.

*Swinburne : A Lecture. By J. W. Mackail. Clarendon Press, 1909.

*A. C. Swinburne : A Critical Study. By Edward Thomas. Martin Secker, 1912.

*Swinburne. By Edmund Gosse. In " Portraits and Sketches." Heinemann, 1913.

Swinburne : An Estimate. By John Drinkwater. Dent, 1913.

Swinburne : A Critical Study. By T. Earle Welby. Elkin Mathews, 1914.

*The Boyhood of A. C. Swinburne. By Mrs. Disney Leith. Chatto & Windus, 1917.

*The Life of Algernon Charles Swinburne. By Edmund Gosse. Macmillan, 1917.

The Letters of A. C. Swinburne : with some Personal Recollections. By Thomas Hake and A. Compton Rickett. John Murray, 1918.

Swinburne and Landor. By W. Drayton Henderson. Macmillan, 1918.

*The Letters of A. C. Swinburne. Edited by Edmund
    Gosse and Thomas Wise.   2 vols.   Heinemann, 1918.
Swinburne as I knew Him.   By Coulson Kernahan.
    John Lane, 1919.
*A Bibliography of the Writings in Prose and Verse of
    A. C. Swinburne.   By Thomas Wise.   2 vols.
    Privately printed, 1919–1920.
*No. 2 The Pines.   By Max Beerbohm.   In " And Even
    Now ".   Heinemann, 1920.
*L'Œuvre de Swinburne.   Par Paul de Reul.   Brussels,
    1922.

INDEX